THE OLD SOW
IN THE
BACK ROOM

THE OLD SOW
IN THE
BACK ROOM

An Englishwoman in Japan

HARRIET SERGEANT

John Murray

Distributed by
Trafalgar Square
North Pomfret, Vermont 05053

First published in 1994
by John Murray (Publishers) Ltd.,
50 Albemarle Street, London W1X 4BD

A catalogue record for this book is available from the British Library

ISBN 0–7195–5173–0

Typeset in 12/14pt Bembo by Wearset, Boldon, Tyne and Wear

Printed and bound in Great Britain by
The University Press, Cambridge

For my husband

1

The first time I visited Japan, I went as a man. Kanebo, a cosmetics company, had invited me, one other journalist and two buyers from the North of England. The others agreed to go on one condition. They had read about the second-class treatment endured by Japanese women. 'You must treat us exactly as you would a delegation of male journalists,' they insisted. The bemused but ever courteous Kanebo did just that.

After speeches of welcome, an exchange of presents and a dinner of alarming formality they escorted us to a club. We entered a private room furnished in white. Ten young women bowed and giggled then drew us down on to the sofas. They popped peanuts into our mouths and dispensed compliments through a translator. The men from Kanebo looked on benignly.

On the way out I had loitered behind when a scream came from the hall. The girls had clustered around one of the buyers, a woman in her fifties with a blue rinse. She was shaking and looking ill. She said that she wanted to fly home immediately. A girl slightly older than the rest and clothed in a bright red dress had propositioned her. 'I have been married twenty-five years,' she insisted almost in tears. Our hosts exchanged puzzled glances. We had asked to be treated like men. Was this not what we expected?

Men, we discovered, led a delightful existence in Japan. Never once did we find ourselves alone. There seemed to be any number of young women available to amuse and care for us. Half a dozen of Kanebo's prettiest employees dressed in the company uniform waved us off when we took the bullet train from Tokyo station. At stops along the route girls bowed deeply, burst into song and presented bouquets before the train pulled out. In Kyoto, the largest of Japan's ancient capitals, fetching employees greeted our party with further armfuls of flowers and escorted us to the hotel. 'Why aren't they doing a proper job?' said the journalist severely to the man from Kanebo. He looked hurt. 'But they are,' he returned. 'They brighten our day. They are known as "the flowers in the office".'

That evening we dined in a geisha house where more women, this time clad in kimono, entertained us in a private room with its own Japanese garden. Even in my hotel bedroom I found a masseuse waiting to massage me to sleep. I thought nothing of this until the masseuse hand strayed. In the old days a father no doubt prepared his son for such an occasion. Mine had not thought to advise his daughter. My eyes flew open. Questions of sexual etiquette rather than erotic urges overwhelmed me. Should I groan, assume a blissful expression or pretend it was not happening? Did I thank the masseuse afterwards? Did she expect a tip? It seemed hardly the service for which I could sign – especially as Kanebo were footing the hotel bill. The masseuse yawned then moved her hand back on to my leg. She was, I realized both tired and bored. 'Please tell me about your famous London fog,' she murmured. I guessed she said that to all the boys.

All the while, our hosts lectured us on Japanese culture. The Japanese were an island race, different and, they implied, superior to the rest of the world. Everything about Japan was different, the weather, the cherry blossom, the diet and especially the Japanese. We nodded earnestly. It was seductive talk. Acceptance of the premise implied intelligence and promised us knowledge with which to impress the uninitiated back home. So we colluded with our hosts. We praised Kyoto as an ancient city even though most of it is ugly and modern. We admired geisha houses despite indifferent food and entertainment more appropriate for children on long car journeys. Our hosts proved peculiarly self-conscious about their culture. They watched our reaction closely. It was not enough that we should enjoy ourselves. We had to do so in a way that reflected well on the Japanese. We had to reassure them all the time as if, without that reassurance, Japanese culture might prove as insubstantial as a cloud and drift off.

On our last night Kanebo decided on a change. They took us to a host bar. In a room decorated in red velvet and ormolu, young men flirted with the wives of Japan's most highly paid executives. After midnight, hostesses and *mama-sans*, in need of spoiling after a hard night spoiling others, took their place. Our escorts sat silent, their hands folded stiffly in their laps. They had never entertained foreigners before. Finally the bravest, with the air of a kamikaze pilot, invited the buyer with the blue rinse to dance. She towered over him, her shoulders and thighs enveloping his slim elegance. The young man stared ahead ignoring the amusement of his colleagues. My escort stiffened his shoulders and led me on to the dance floor. 'One, two, one, two, three,' he intoned, frowning at my wayward feet. 'Do you dance the rock and roll?' I enquired. His frown deepened. I noticed he was wearing mascara and rouge. Suddenly he thrust me backwards. When I stumbled, he steadied me reproachfully then resumed his intonation. It was the only English he knew. Helpless in the arms of this clockwork boy I sought to fathom the tango, Japanese style.

So ended my first visit to Japan. I had seen a land of cherry blossom and geisha. The Japan, in other words, that Japanese like to show visitors. The Japan most people think of, when they think about the country. Like many before me, I believed that I had seen the real Japan. I failed to understand it was not Japan at all but an artificial creation preserved to impress foreigners and only experienced by ordinary Japanese on television or expense accounts.

The next time I returned to Japan as a woman, worse, as a wife and mother. The Japanese have a term for it: *kanae*, 'her indoors' or what they used to call *zashiki buta*, 'the old sow in the back room'. I had come to live on and off for six and a half years in the country. I soon discovered that Japan is a manufacturer not only of

9

goods but also of myths to which the West has proved equally susceptible. I read books about Japan's takeover of the world, about Zen, geisha or affairs with inscrutable bar girls, but I found nothing on what I now experienced. As a woman in Japan you do not count. No one is interested in selling you a myth or putting on a show. It means that while the foreign male sits transfixed, you can slip behind the scenes and join the cast, kimono loosened, drinking beer and chewing dried octopus in the green room. It is this backstage Japan that I began to explore.

I moved with my husband and small daughter to Shirogane, the Holland Park of Tokyo. Like many of the city's neighbourhoods, one block behind the futuristic skyscrapers and overpasses hung with giant video screens, old ladies in kimono hobbled down lanes cluttered with temples, wooden houses and plots of morning glory. The price of land ensured that even the modest two- or three-bedroom houses in our street belonged to Tokyo's wealthiest. In my lane lived a former geisha, the owner of a construction company, two retired gangsters and a child movie star. All the houses exuded secrecy. High walls surrounded tiny gardens. Shoji screens or bars blocked the windows. You could not see in or out.

At first I hated Tokyo. It was so clean, ordered and ugly. Window cleaners wore white gloves, taxi drivers refused tips and dog shit was collected even as it fell. I felt like a child with a strict parent. I was always in the wrong place at the wrong time doing the wrong thing. Even the simplest activity led to conflict or confusion, as I discovered when I went swimming.

I was surprised to learn that a public swimming bath existed at all. I first arrived in Japan in 1986. At that time Tokyo's ward offices were spending their income on palatial head offices. Tax payers were left to fend for themselves. Tokyoites, however, had begun to demand better things of their city. Playgrounds were starting to be built and trees to be planted. I wondered if workshops and consumer associations would appear next. Was civic indulgence the first step to Western decadence? My local swimming pool seemed the place to find out.

The sports centre was a large modern building surrounded by cherry trees. A bent old man sold me a ticket and showed me where to leave my shoes. In the women's changing room a recorded voice issued instructions and encouragement. I found myself in need of both. Undressing is a serious business in Japan. Like every Japanese activity it requires the right equipment and a proper attitude. Around me Japanese women performed a series of twists, shakes and jerks beneath towels designed to conceal. Elasticated at the neck and reaching to the knee, they stopped me discovering exactly what about the Japanese female so excites the foreign male. Perhaps it is the quantity of Japanese underwear. In a hot, humid month where even a short walk drenched shirts, the girl next to me had on a petticoat, a slip, a bra, two girdles and a pair of support tights. The matrons drew in their breath as I removed my tee-shirt. A pair of Marks & Spencer knickers does not win you friends in a Tokyo changing room.

Neither did my one-piece swimming costume. The matrons glanced at me and nudged each other. Meanwhile, my neighbour, her underwear folded and put away, wriggled into yet another bra and pants. Over this she slipped a polka-dot bikini. An old lady came in and stared at me. 'Why is that foreigner wearing nothing under her costume,' she asked the others. 'She doesn't know any better,' said one shaking her head. Underdressed but undaunted I followed Miss Polka Dot to the swimming pool.

Even a Tokyo rush hour had not prepared me. In the shallow end children splashed, women stood in groups gossiping, and old men stared into space or at the nearest pretty girl. At the deep end young men queued up to swim a lap. At their turn they threw themselves into a brief spasm of butterfly before joining another queue for the swim back. I could barely glimpse water for people.

I had just reached the poolside when a volley of whistles filled the air. Four young life guards in red caps and brief red costumes (the underwear rule does not apply to Japanese men) glared at me from their high chairs. Why was I not wetter, they demanded in mime. Obviously I had not showered properly. I walked back to

11

the showers and returned, dutifully wet. Once again the whistles ambushed me. Had I showered my hair, they mimed again. Guiltily I removed my cap. Underneath my hair was dry. I returned to the showers, showered my hair, put on my cap over my wet hair, showered my cap then returned to the pool. This time I got as far as the shallow end. The guards pointed to my goggles. Foreign, they exclaimed, likely to cause injury to other swimmers and forbidden in Japanese pools. Meekly I took off my goggles and joined the queue for a swim.

Swimming pool etiquette in Japan is applicable to Japanese life in general. You do not queue jump, you cannot overtake and, if you do collide with someone else, both swimmers must stop and tread water while executing a bow. I broke all three rules when I swam into the stomach of a sumo wrestler. He was playing ball with two other sumo wrestlers in the centre of the pool. Each weighed about twenty-five stone, wore capacious trunks in bright colours and had his hair smoothed into a top knot. About them floated shoals of children in rubber rings. When I tried to swim around the wrestler he bounced the beach ball on my head. I looked up over the stomach to the moon face above me. The moment had come, I decided, to practise my first aquatic bow.

In between waiting my turn and apologizing for this and other misdemeanours I accomplished three laps in ten minutes. I was on my fourth lap when the pool started to empty. People climbed out and sat on benches lining the walls. Soon I was the only person left. For the first time I began to enjoy myself. I had even started to crawl when the whistles shrilled. One of the guards climbed down from the high chair, swaggered over to the pool's edge and jerked his head at me. Without looking at him, I swam on. At the other end, a second guard leant forward from his chair. 'Get out!' he hissed. I smiled vaguely and set off on another length. The crowd watched in silence. 'Rest Time, Rest Time,' shouted the first guard. He crouched down at the edge of the pool and made a grab at me. I kicked out of his reach. At the other end the second guard was preparing to wade in after me. I ignored him and set off on the return lap, only to find the first guard now in the water and very cross indeed. Japanese officials, however lowly, are accustomed to obedience, especially from women. 'Rest Time!' he ejected. I stopped, stood up and said in English that if I wanted to rest I would not have come swimming. The crowd sucked in its breath. 'Out, OUT,' shouted the guard. I thought he might hit me. The crowd, still silent, pretended not to look. The guard now jabbed at me, as one might a beast of uncertain temperament. Reluctantly I turned towards the steps, adjusted my costume to compensate for my lack of underwear, then climbed out of the pool. An old lady made room for me on a bench. After a moment she said in halting English, 'This is Rest Time. The guards stand in for our mother. When they see we are tired they tell us to rest.'

Half an hour later the pool had to be emptied again. I walked up and down, shivering ostentatiously. The same old lady offered me a towel. This, she explained, was Clean Up Time. Every two and a half hours the swimming pool closed for an hour. The four guards appeared wearing masks, snorkels and flippers and dived into the empty pool. After ten minutes they climbed out and lined up together. In one hand they held the result of their swim, sticking plasters, hair pins, nests of black hair. With the other they removed their headgear, tucked it under their arm and, still in unison, bowed to the departing crowds. Wet, if nothing else, I made my way to the changing room.

'You can't take on the whole Japanese nation,' said my husband when I complained. Our experience of Japan was proving very different. Japanese women treated him with respect. Japanese men disliked me on sight. Young Japanese befriended me briefly like an exotic pet bought on impulse and then regretted. Older Japanese, enraged at my apparent lack of respect, would have nothing to do with me. Humiliation turned into paranoia about everything Japanese. Was this, I wondered, what black people felt in a white society? Some days I could take no more. The compulsion to behave badly overwhelmed me. To knowing glances from the Japanese, I threw tantrums in public places. They had heard how foreigners behaved, I merely confirmed their prejudices.

Finally my neighbour invited me to lunch. We met when I

stopped to admire her roses. They fell like a wave over her garden wall. In a fit of homesickness I had paused to smell them. Then I lifted up my eighteen-month old daughter, who promptly burst into tears. The front door opened to reveal a middle-aged lady with a voluptuous figure encased in cashmere. I summoned up two months of Japanese lessons and said, 'This is an English flower.' My neighbour retorted in English, 'Yes and they are not for picking!' She then fetched a rice cake for my daughter. Gabriella sucked it greedily. 'She likes Japanese things!' said my neighbour with satisfaction and introduced herself as Mrs Abe.

Her lunch party was my initiation ceremony to the neighbourhood. Up until then I had bowed to my neighbours and even mastered the rules governing rubbish collection, a frequent source of conflict between foreigners and Japanese. But now I had to pass the acceptance test inside a Japanese home. Inside and outside are very different in Japan. 'You'll never succeed,' warned a French friend. 'Eat a sandwich before you go,' advised an American.

My French friend took me to buy the present. 'You won't get past the front door without one,' she said. In Japan present giving has nothing to do with the present itself. What counts is where it came from and how much it cost. I bought mine in a famous store. It was very expensive and beautifully wrapped. 'The wrapping is the most important thing,' said my friend. The same applied to me. She made me wear my one designer cocktail dress – 'Japanese women dress up at lunch time' – and white tights. They should have been lacy but I rebelled. Thus equipped, I set out for the unknown of the Japanese home.

Mrs Abe met me at the door. I bowed, held my head down for the count of three, raised it slowly and, as my eyes met hers, handed over the present. Mrs Abe bowed in return. Flushed with success, I tackled the shoe test.

Japanese never wear shoes inside the home. Footwear is left in the hall, one step down from the rest of the house. Every Japanese, from small children to removal men carrying grand pianos, slide out of their shoes and on to the step in a single movement, leaving their shoes neatly aligned and facing the front door. Mrs Abe watched me fail with interest. She then offered me a pair of slippers. They had high heels and barely covered half my foot. A fluffy rabbit's head decorated each toe. They did nothing for the cocktail dress.

Despite belonging to one of Japan's oldest and most eminent families, Mrs Abe lived in a home half the size of an English council house and jerry built. The drains smelt and the ceilings were low. I had imagined something as elegant and daunting as Mrs Abe herself. Instead heavy Edwardian furniture, a stuffed deer's head and an Art Deco lamp jostled unhappily with a collection of Japanese dolls. The perfect use of space characteristic of traditional Japanese interiors deserts the Japanese when faced with Western objects. So, apparently, do Japanese notions of cleanliness. Everything looked in need of a dusting. Mrs Abe pointed to a painting of the Lake District, 'That's from Harrods,' she said proudly.

She introduced me to two middle-aged Japanese ladies who lived nearby. They both wore sprays of jewellery and lacy tights. We sat down to lunch. Mrs Abe presented each of us with a lacquer box dived into three tiers, each tier concealing minute portions of food. I now understand the point of the sandwich. The ladies picked at their food. I attacked the largest piece which turned out to be an ice cube surmounted by four fish eggs. Mrs Abe explained the dishes. 'We Japanese prefer seasonal food,' she said to me. 'We are the only country in the world with four seasons.' Ignoring my suggestion that Britain too might have four seasons, Mrs Abe only wanted to hear how Japan differed from other countries. I upset her when I successfully picked up a bean with my chopsticks. 'Do people use chopsticks outside Japan?' she asked incredulously. It was, I realized, the wrong test to pass.

My examination now moved from the practical to the personal. The ladies were discussing their hobbies. Mrs Abe attended tea ceremony classes, one lady studied the art of putting on a kimono, the other, Japanese cookery. 'What is your hobby?' they asked. Desperately I tried to think of one. 'She writes books,' said Mrs Abe. Her friends looked unimpressed. One said, 'If I had time, I would like to write a book.' The other explained, 'Japanese women are expected to put their family first.' They exchanged stories of domestic self-sacrifice to which I found myself unable to contribute. Mrs Abe easily triumphed with the tale of her father-in-law. When he went to hospital for an operation, he refused to let the nurses touch him. Instead his wife, daughter and daughter-in-law had to nurse him, each woman taking an eight-hour shift. After two weeks Mrs Abe collapsed with nervous exhaustion and was admitted to the same hospital.

'Things are different in England,' I said weakly. 'She has a nanny,' said Mrs Abe in a voice which suggested I kept a dangerous animal. The ladies looked amazed. One said, 'We Japanese take care of our own children, however rich the family.' I wondered what happened when they went out at night. 'Japanese women do not go out,' they informed me. Neither of Mrs Abe's friends had ever been to a restaurant with their husbands in the evening. The widowed Mrs Abe had only accompanied her husband when he entertained foreigners. One lady added, 'My husband rings up every night to check I am at home.' It seemed their only form of communication. During the week he returned in the small hours after a hard night of business entertainment. On Saturday he played golf and on Sunday he slept. 'A good husband is healthy and absent,' said Mrs Abe quoting a Japanese proverb.

I sat, knees pressed together, holding my tea cup in the approved manner and feeling increasingly absurd, but worse was yet to come. One lady was describing her school reunion party. A former classmate had asked, 'What are you doing now? Golf, tennis or boyfriends?' I thought I had misheard when Mrs Abe turned to me and said, 'All Japanese wives have lovers. Our husbands can't complain because of their own behaviour.' 'Do you have a lover?' asked her friend conversationally. Three expectant faces turned to me. In this, at least, they thought, I would excel. I saw they anticipated something more exotic than the usual, a Cherokee Indian or an Ethiopian prince perhaps. Shame overwhelmed me. I was about to fail this test as surely as the others. In a small voice I admitted that I was still keen on my husband. The ladies exchanged glances. I did not need a translation. I would not be asked again.

However alien I found Mrs Abe, she had at least offered me the chance of a social life of sorts. Her friends were not exaggerating. Husbands and wives did indeed lead separate lives in Japan. When we invited Japanese couples to dinner either both dropped out at the last minute or the husband came alone. I rarely saw my own husband. He worked until ten o'clock each night or attended business dinners. Three times a week Japanese companies entertained him in establishments which only those on expense accounts could enjoy. One night I too was invited. The Japanese company, keen to appear international, had included wives in the invitation. At the restaurant a kimono-clad waitress showed us to a private room. The Japanese company put the wives at one end of the table, themselves at the other. The wives reacted grumpily to my attempts at conversation. They had not wanted to come out. It upset their routine. One was missing her favourite television programme. 'My husband will have to do something to make up for it,' she added. The others all nodded with satisfaction, 'Oh yes, they're in our debt all right,' they agreed. The restaurant served a series of courses known as *kaiseki*. I explained to my neighbour that I had never tried *kaiseki* before and asked her help. She looked amazed. 'I have no idea,' she said. 'This is the first time I have ever eaten in a restaurant with my husband.' She was in her fifties.

The geishas and tea ceremonies I had enjoyed on my first visit to Japan appeared another world now. As a couple we could not afford them. Japanese culture is an expensive business. Owning race horses or a yacht is cheap in comparison. Traditional Japan is as much a never-never land to the ordinary Japanese as it is to the foreigner. Only when the company pays can they enjoy it. Japanese companies spend more on corporate entertainment than they do on share dividends, but rarely do they extend it to wives. So when a Japanese company invited us both for the weekend, I could hardly believe my luck.

A company car complete with new, white seat covers and a

17

driver in white gloves took us to the *ryokan*, a traditional Japanese inn outside Tokyo. On the way my husband gave me a lecture on *ryokan* etiquette. As a man and a banker, he had already experienced more of Japanese life than I had. 'I don't want you embarrassing me,' he warned. I said it did not sound a relaxing weekend. 'Japanese can be very informal,' he replied. 'You just have to know when.'

The *ryokan* stood in a suburb of *pachinko* parlours (amusement arcades) and small factories, surrounded by a high wall. We stepped through the gate and left modern Japan behind. Pine and plum trees shaded the courtyard. The *ryokan* itself was an old, wooden structure with a roof that curled at the edges. At the entrance we took off our shoes on a stone slab. Japanese maids lined up to welcome us, their kimonos bright spots in the gloom. Through a series of half-open shoji (paper) screens, I glimpsed maple leaves and the stone lantern of a Japanese garden. Like all really expensive establishments, the *ryokan* appeared empty but for ourselves. In the hall Mr Sato, a director of our host company, introduced himself. He suggested we first have a bath, 'so as to get to know each other'. After washing and rinsing themselves, the Japanese soak together in a hot tub or *ofuro*. 'Very traditional, very relaxing,' promised Mr Sato adding to me, 'The wives of our company directors are waiting for you in the ladies' *ofuro*.' I looked helplessly at my husband. Meeting a group of Japanese ladies is daunting enough without being naked.

The ladies' *ofuro* was made of stone and was the size of a small swimming pool. Set in the wall enclosing the area were a series of hand showers. In front of each stood a bamboo bucket and stool. Four Japanese ladies lay up to their chins in the steaming water. All watched attentively as I began to wash. Japanese believe that a foreigner can never wash too much but rarely does. Forewarned of this I sat on the doll-sized stool and soaped myself from neck to toe. All went well until I reached my bottom. Then I panicked. I recalled no instructions for washing bottoms. Was I meant to stand up, crouch or in some way use the hole placed in the centre of the stool? Did cleanliness take precedence over modesty or vice versa?

I chose cleanliness. The Japanese ladies averted their eyes but nodded approvingly when I stepped into the *ofuro*. There followed a fleeting moment of ease and pleasure before a fresh dilemma arose: did one chat in an *ofuro*? My neighbour responded firmly to my efforts. 'Westerners hate silence, don't they,' she said. 'We Japanese do not feel the need to talk all the time. We enjoy the peace.' She lay back and closed her eyes. I stared through the window at the formal Japanese garden where not a pebble had been laid or a branch allowed to bud without forethought. Then with my face turning red, my head perspiring and the ordeal of dinner yet to come I tried, very hard, to enjoy myself.

Mr Sato was waiting in our room. 'Dinner in ten minutes,' he said cheerfully. It was not yet six o'clock and I was wearing *yukata*, the blue and white cotton robe provided by the *ryokan* to put on after bathing. I explained that I had to change. 'Change?' said a perplexed Mr Sato. 'Everyone is wearing *yukata*. It is Japanese tradition.' This sudden switch to informality unnerved me. I had brought my party dress and felt in need of it. I was unsure I could face a formal Japanese dinner in my dressing gown. How far did this informality go? Should I, for example, make up my face – and what about jewellery? Large, sparkling earrings seemed hardly the thing with a cotton kimono. 'I am not happy at all,' I said to my husband as we left the room.

Outside our maid knelt, head bowed, hands folded in front of her knees. Then she saw me. 'You are wearing your *yukata* like a corpse,' she said in horror, jumping to her feet. Before I could protest, she had untied my sash and opened my robe much to the interest of Mr Sato. She then rewrapped me, folding the material tight around my body from the neck down. The strange appearance of my husband she ignored. At six foot four and a good eight inches taller than the average Japanese, his *yukata* barely reached his knees. There followed an expanse of hairy leg then plastic slippers. 'Men', said Mr Sato, 'can wear it as they like.'

The maid showed us into a vast room, floored with tatami (rice straw) matting. The screens on one side were drawn back to reveal the garden. We ate at a low lacquer table seated on cushions. The

President of the Japanese company sat half-way along the table, his colleagues and their wives arranged either side of him. The foreigners positioned themselves opposite. The dinner followed the pattern of all Japanese business dinners. We discussed the weather, the names of our children and the food. A nervous giggle from the Japanese introduced more daring subjects for conversation, such as what foreigners thought of Japanese customs like sleeping on the floor and using chopsticks.

All the while, four middle-aged women in kimono poured sake and lit cigarettes. They wore white make-up and elaborate pins in their hair. Their kimono slipped away from their shoulders to reveal a glimpse of white, powdered neck. The oldest, who was in her seventies, sat in a corner and played the samisen, a Japanese guitar of three strings plucked with a plectrum. 'Geisha', whispered my husband,' aren't all young, beautiful and languid.' These women cracked jokes and robustly clapped my husband on the shoulder. 'They are probably charging £1000 each for tonight,' he added. Their purpose, like that of the *ofuro* and the garden, was to relax us. As if by prearranged signal their good-time aura became the order of the evening. We began to laugh. Mr Sato asked if I had ever been an air hostess. The geisha admired my husband's legs. We exchanged toasts, professed friendship and the desire to meet again. The aim of the dinner now accomplished, the President stood up. He was returning to Tokyo in order to play golf the next day with other clients. 'I was just beginning to have fun,' I said to my husband as we waved him off.

On the way to bed I found the geisha and the company wives seated in the television room. 'We have never been allowed to meet geisha before,' explained Mr Sato's wife. 'Our husbands usually keep us apart. They are telling us all about face packs,' she added. I sat down with them. The talk switched to men. The group roared with laughter, 'Oh, I can't translate that,' spluttered Mrs Sato. Somebody ordered more sake. The samisen player told me she had a daughter living in Brighton. The geisha lit their own cigarettes and blew smoke rings before starting on more anecdotes. Perhaps it was the sake, but for the first time that weekend, I began really to enjoy myself.

My attempts to get around Tokyo proved as confusing as trying to understand the Japanese. Most of Tokyo was rebuilt during the years of poverty after the Second World War. It left the city with a makeshift air, of waterways hastily filled in and buildings knocked up from the cheapest materials. There are no vistas and few parks. Streets stretch in every direction, an interminable tangle of overhead cables, billboards and cramped, shabby dwellings fronted by bars and frosted glass. At the heart of the city lies the Imperial Palace. Crowded streets suddenly give way to a moat and steep, wooded slopes. The sudden eruption of space and greenery elates the senses. One emerges from prison. There is the glint of water and the sun shines. Sections of wall made up of giant blocks of granite and volcanic rock surge unevenly upwards.

At each corner of the wall stones the size of a man tilt like clenched fists into the sky. This thumbing at fate is all that remains of one of the largest fortified palaces in the world. In 1590, after years of civil war, the victor, Toyotomi Hideyoshi, offered his most powerful ally, Tokugawa Ieyasu, the eight provinces of the east which included Edo or modern-day Tokyo. Ieyasu set out to transform the town surrounded by wetlands into an imaginative fortification. New advances in engineering allowed him to turn the marsh into a spiral of moats with the castle at its centre. Feudal lords eager to prove their loyalty provided men, money and boats to transport blocks of stone from the cliffs of Izu Peninsula over a hundred kilometres away. After the sea journey, teams of a hundred men or more, cheered on by groups of entertainers, dancing, banging drums and blowing conch shells, hauled the rocks on sledges laid on paths of seaweed. They erected a keep, several fortresses and fortified gates and thirty-six look-out towers to guard the bridges over the moats.

Most of that has long gone, destroyed by earthquakes, fires and American bombers. Behind the wall now lie some disappointing buildings dating from the 1950s where the Emperor and his family live. The emphasis is all on the fortification. As you walk around the rather dull Imperial Gardens beyond, it strikes you that this is also true of Japan. The Japanese have surrounded their institutions, their culture and themselves with a series of earthworks. Life for the foreigner takes on the characteristics of siege warfare. As soon as you penetrate one barrier, you are presented with another. Sometimes you wonder if the whole point of Japan is the wall itself rather than the treasure inside. The Japanese give the impression of fearing that, their defences breached, they will prove as unsatisfactory as the tarmac paths and 'Keep Off the Grass' signs of the Imperial Gardens.

Motorways and office buildings have replaced most of Toku- gawa Ieyasu's moats but his method of defence continues to protect the city from the curious foreigner. Again and again I was reminded of those sinuous, frustrating waterways as I tried to find my way around Tokyo. There are few street names. Houses are numbered according to when they were built rather than sequen- tially. Every neighbourhood is made up of a block of dwellings that wraps inwards like a snail's shell. Baffled Japanese study the neighbourhood map painted on a sheet of tin and displaying each house with its owner's name. For foreigners who cannot read Japanese the outlook is desperate. Japanese avoided me when I sought help. If I did manage to stop someone, they turned the map around several times, sucked their teeth, shook their heads and expressed total bewilderment at anything more than a street away.

The foreigner learns to approach Tokyo not as a city but as a jungle or desert. I never left home without two or three maps (invitations, whether from a business, a shop or a party, always arrive with one), a Japanese language dictionary, the name of my destination written in Japanese (Japanese are nonplussed by even the most subtle mispronunciation) and the telephone number of where I was going. It was also vital to take note of my route for the journey back. Once I met a foreign woman crying in the street. She had moved in the day before and just popped out to buy milk. 'Now I can't find my way home,' she wailed. 'I've been trying for half an hour.' Tokyoites navigate by landmarks, a striking skyscraper, a crossing or a peculiar pink coffee shop. Unfortunately Tokyo is in constant upheaval. Buildings are pulled down in a day. Just as I began to feel safe, a precious landmark would disappear behind white plastic curtains, several stories high. After a month the curtains opened to reveal a quite different building or sometimes the fresh tarmac of a new car park.

Getting lost is the best way of getting to know a city. I started with my own neighbourhood. We lived on one of the innumerable small hills that dot Tokyo. The streets were very narrow, often no more than lanes with houses and apartment blocks scaled down accordingly. A number of traditional wooden Japanese homes remained. Some were quite large, surrounded by gardens planted with carefully pruned magnolia and cherry trees. Others proved minute. I passed one every day screened by bushes. Through the foliage I glimpsed a Japanese garden with stone slabs embedded in moss leading to a tiny wooden house. Some mornings the shoji screen stood open to reveal an old lady in kimono kneeling at the entrance. In winter she wore a rug over her knees. A neighbour often stopped at the gate for a chat. The house and garden seemed too small for even a Japanese to enter. I imagined her sitting there hour after hour, stirring only in the evening to prepare rice and unroll her futon. I never caught sight of anything practical or modern like a bathroom or a radio. The old woman became my talisman. If I glimpsed her through the trees first thing, the day promised well. On those mornings when the shoji screen remained closed, I wanted to pause and leave an offering, a saucer of peaches or a peony.

At the bottom of the hill lay a shopping street. The owners had joined together to install a tannoy system which played bird song interspersed with public announcements and Frank Sinatra. I once complained about the noise to the fishmonger. He reproved, 'Nobody likes silence. People might feel lonely as they walk along.' From the lampposts arched sprays of plastic flowers. These changed according to the season. In spring the street sported pink and white plastic blossom. Summer's fake irises gave way to tinkling autumnal leaves which in turn were replaced by a Christmas wreath of bells and fir cones. These last were, at least, authentic.

Behind the shopping street ran lanes crammed with small factories, minute children's playgrounds and older, wooden shops. Early in the morning housewives appeared at their front door equipped with brush and dustpan to sweep the area of pavement that lay immediately in front of their home. Clutter from inside their tiny houses seeped on to the pavement. Air conditioning units, washing machines, brooms, pails and even wash rags lived permanently out of doors. They never appeared to be stolen. A profusion of flowers, shrubs and small trees planted in every size of plastic pot, polyurethane box or tin can were stacked on the air conditioning units and overflowed the pavement. The effect of this scaled-down city was to make me feel large and awkward. I was constantly tripping over or breaking things.

Many of the shops were run by old couples in order to provide themselves with a pension and a retirement hobby. They lived in a tatami room at the back separated from the store by a step and shoji screens. They made tatami mats or sold fresh bean curd stored in wooden barrels of water. The most decrepit of the wooden shacks housed my drycleaner. The owner was a tall, old woman fond of purple tracksuits. Her female neighbours disapproved of her. Certainly I had never seen Mrs Kato with a dustpan and brush. She never did anything domestic at all, preferring to stroll about the neighbourhood exercising her Pyrenean mountain dog. Occasionally, she paused to discuss the animal's health or show off its points. She left the shop in the charge of her son, a large, shambling man dressed, whatever the season, in a vest, pants and sandals. On his mother's return he would hurry from the back to open the gate next to the counter. She would sniff, say something sharp, then busy herself wiping the dog's feet.

Mrs Kato beamed on my arrival and chatted to my daughter. Sometimes she stuffed money back into my hand saying, 'Have this one on us.' Then drawing close, she feigned a fear of her son, adding, 'But don't tell him!' I assumed no other foreigner entered the rickety drycleaner. Even so Mrs Kato's son always stared at me blankly when I pushed open the sliding door until I said my name. Then he too exclaimed with pleasure and offered me a reduction. 'This our secret?' he whispered, glancing uneasily at the back where his mother was preparing dog food. One day he hesitated, staring hard out of wet, red-rimmed eyes, 'Mrs Sloane?' he asked tentatively. Mrs Sloane, it turned out, received a bigger reduction than me.

At least once a month a wooden house or shop disappeared; packed up and pulled down in an afternoon. Modern homes turned over with equal rapidity. Every ten years houses were rebuilt or transformed into a block of flats. Even as I grew to know and like my neighbourhood, it vanished. This is true of Japan generally. Japanese extol the past as they destroy it. Tokyoites revere tradition in a metropolis whose only constant feature since its founding in 1590 has been its rate of change. Earthquakes and fires have regularly devastated the city. In this century alone Tokyo suffered from the Great Kanto earthquake in 1923 and the American bombing raids of 1945. The latter drove out or killed 60 per cent of Tokyo's population and levelled the city. Not until the 1960s did many central wards return to their pre-war population. Neighbourhoods which give the impression of long duration date from after the Second World War. Festivals described as historical started a mere forty years ago and are added to and altered each year. This sense of impermanence is the backdrop to life in Tokyo. Even now the city waits for a major earthquake already overdue. A slight tremble underfoot and an eerie silence amongst Tokyo's crow population saw me under the kitchen table clutching my child, convinced that it had begun.

Despite the vastness of the city, Tokyo's main thoroughfares were built on the same doll's-house scale as the lanes. Even the skyscrapers had a Toy Town eccentricity. Many were only one window wide. Every floor offered a different shop, restaurant or nightclub, their names extending down the side of the building like brightly coloured flags. There were no broad vistas or avenues. Nothing appeared planned. Whimsical design set each skyscraper apart from its neighbour. One boasting stained glass windows and Art Deco balconies might have as its neighbour an apartment block draped with a veil of steel from which peeped bamboo foliage. The streets themselves exuded the same Toy Town air – the pavements and the people squeaky clean and everybody dressed in their best. Only young mothers seemed to leave home casually clothed and without make-up. Japanese women always wore tights, even in the heat of summer, and appeared fresh from the hairdresser. They giggled beside their perfectly turned out escorts, a regiment of Barbie dolls on a date.

Like its skyscrapers, Tokyo possessed level upon level of bizarrely juxtaposed activity. Extraordinary experiences were on offer if I could only work out which buttons to press. The drabness of most people's lives had forced numerous blooms of eccentricity. On my first day in Tokyo I inevitably got lost. At length I came to an overpass beneath which someone had erected an enclosure. A pack of beagles rose up and bayed at me. They had been feasting on the carcass of a deer, its hooves and horns still recognizable amongst the bloody flesh. Who kept such hounds in central Tokyo? Where had they found a deer on which to feed them? This surreal sight summed up the mood of those first few months. I had travelled in China and the Far East. I had lived in America and Southern Africa, but my journey to Japan might as well have been to the moon or Mars, so alien did I feel. I stared in bewilderment until an elderly foreigner turned the corner. After giving me directions, he asked how long I had lived in Japan. 'It's my first week,' I replied. He had arrived with the American occupational forces forty years ago that month. He had stayed ever since. He said, 'You will be quite happy here as long as you don't try to belong.'

Mrs Abe relented over my disappointing lack of lovers and asked me back to tea. Two other ladies joined us. Mrs Tashiro, plump and bejewelled, was the wife of an eminent politician. The other lady proved to be the wife of the President of one of Japan's largest banks. The night before I had dined with her American counter-part. The contrast was striking. No one could describe Mrs Kobayashi as a trophy wife. Short and dumpy with a homely face, she had never been abroad. Her husband always left her behind. I described my encounter with the geisha. They were fascinated. Mrs Kobayashi recalled making a disparaging remark to her husband on the subject. He had retorted, 'Geisha are much better educated than you!' The three women shook their heads. They envied not so much the geishas' erotic appeal as their intelligence and ability to converse. Mrs Kobayashi said sharply, 'If I had nothing to do all day, I would have learnt to play the samisen by now!'

Mrs Abe now produced the largest apple I had ever seen. She served slices of it to us on tooth picks. Naturally this proved no ordinary fruit but one grown in the garden of Mrs Abe's country house and sent up for the occasion. We murmured our apprecia-tion. Mrs Abe said that I should visit the Japanese countryside. 'We Japanese love nature,' she added in a tone implying that no one else could. I mentioned that I was going skiing at the weekend. 'Who will take care of your child?' they exclaimed. Skiing was a down-market activity only enjoyed by students and secretaries they added. Married couples never went. We looked at each other. The tea appeared to be going as badly as the lunch. Mrs Abe hesitated a moment and then asked me to describe my last trip to China. 'She travels without her husband,' she said to the others. They leaned forward eagerly. After a number of anecdotes, they stopped laughing, dabbed their eyes and exchanged glances. Mrs Kobayashi gave an imperceptible nod. Mrs Abe explained that the three of them lunched regularly together. Perhaps I might care to join them? Elated by this surprising offer of friendship I left the city that weekend with a light heart.

Sheer numbers of Japanese departing at the weekend turn any expedition from Tokyo into an ordeal. It took us three hours by train and a forty-minute taxi ride before we glimpsed our hotel, a shabby, modern building at the foot of the Japan Alps. On the way

27

I had seen not Mrs Abe's vaunted countryside but mile upon mile of urban sprawl. When we finally emerged into fields and mountains not a hundred yards passed without a factory, gravel pit, cheap hotel or car dump appearing through the trees. Mrs Abe had sold me another myth.

The farmer who originally owned the land now ran the hotel with his family. He was astounded when our party asked for separate rooms. Futons laid out on tatami mats allow an infinite number of Japanese to sleep in one place. 'Charge by room, not person,' he explained. He looked at us, three couples, three children under the age of three and a nanny. 'Wouldn't you be much happier together?' he asked.

At seven thirty loudspeakers in the corridor announced breakfast. We ate with fifty other people in an institutional-sized dining room. The farmer's family had risen at five to lay out trays of rice, raw egg, dried seaweed and pickles on rows of tables. I asked for a cup of coffee. 'Japanese tea only,' said the grandfather. Afterwards the farmer's wife and her sister came to the door to see us off. 'You always get service if nothing else,' said my husband.

Outside four ski slopes rose above our hotel. The noise was extraordinary. It was as if the Japanese, finding themselves outside a city, had done everything possible to rectify the situation. Loudspeakers fixed to the chair lifts blared waltzes across the slopes. A snow plough burst into Greensleeves whenever it reversed and the lavatory rolls in a mountain café tinkled out a Scottish air. Even this was not enough for one couple who wore a headphone and mouthpiece designed, I imagined, to fill that rare moment of silence with an exchange on the weather or the next turn.

The slopes were gentle, short and dangerous. The sheer number of skiers made it impossible to find a bump to turn on without being hit. Young men, released from the strictures of city life, hurled themselves past me. Girls, in the business to be admired, took a more leisurely line. They displayed new and expensive white suits slashed with purple, white boots with pink and purple clips and white skis. Long hair spilling over the shoulders appeared the vital accessory. Even in the worst blizzards they refused to wear a hat, preferring to let the snow gather then freeze on their hair. They were heavily made-up and delighted in fluffy ear muffs, hence their name, 'Snow Bunnies'. I had taken refuge under a tree when a Snow Bunny made straight for me. She tipped over, her head down with her bottom wriggling in my direction, all the time emitting excited shrieks. I shrieked back. The effect was instantaneous. The Snow Bunny went suddenly still then scrambled to her feet and made off as if I did not exist and the incident had never taken place. It was only after my fourth such encounter that I realized what was happening. In my unfashionable anorak and hat, the Snow Bunnies had mistaken me for a foreign man. After that I stopped off to buy my own pair of fluffy ear muffs.

When not avoiding Snow Bunnies, I stood in queues. A five-minute ski required twenty minutes of queuing. The Japanese, unlike the British, refuse to make a line but nor do they enjoy the vicious free for all of the French. Japanese queues work by osmosis. Nobody looks at each other, pokes their neighbour's calf with ski sticks or makes loud comments about 'les sâles Anglaises'. People seem to know by instinct who should pass through first. This also means they know which Westerner (Japanese do not queue jump unless they have been to an American university) has moved out of turn and by how much. They do not try to stop the offender. A few Japanese men nod their heads indulgently as if at a naughty child. 'It's not much fun when everyone knows what you are doing,' I complained to my husband.

At the head of the queue stood the lift men. They were retired farm workers with red, weathered faces incongruously dressed in brightly coloured anoraks with padded shoulders. In the brief moment of contact they cocooned each skier with care. One swept the snow from the seat with a new brush. Another raised his baton with its furled, red flag to indicate that the next couple might go. A third even waded up the hill to pick up my fallen glove, handed it to the people in the chair behind and, still thigh deep in snow, bowed to me until I was out of sight. A fourth made himself less welcome. In pursuit of solitude and safety, I had found

29

a strip of powder snow to the side of the piste. As I made my first turn a man's voice abruptly replaced 'The Blue Danube' on the megaphones attached to the chair lift. He shouted at me to return and, when I took no notice, pursued me vocally down the slope with a lecture on piste safety.

At the end of the day we skied to an *onsen*. Naked Japanese with wash rags on their heads lay in the hot spring water surrounded by snow. This looked very inviting until I realized undressing also took place in the open air. There is nothing seductive about aged polo neck jerseys, yellowing vests, tights with holes, a grey bra and goose pimples. Shivering with cold and shame I climbed into the *onsen*. I looked up expecting, as the only foreign woman, all eyes to be upon me. Instead everyone was staring at my husband. 'Look at his chest!' hissed one Japanese woman to her husband. Casually he glanced over then sucked his teeth. 'It's a door mat!' he said stupefied.

Back at the hotel I had just climbed into my bath when loudspeakers again disturbed me, this time with a summons to dinner. It proved identical to breakfast except for a cold hamburger. That night we slept in Japanese fashion on futons laid out on the floor, our daughter between us. My husband thought it cosy. 'Japanese parents always sleep with their children. Perhaps we should do this more often,' he said before turning off the light and falling instantly asleep. My daughter, enchanted to have me at arm's reach, woke up every two hours. In between I dreamt of hot chocolate, *tarte aux pommes* and French ski instructors.

After that it proved a relief to return to Tokyo. Unlike the Japanese I know that I do not like the countryside.

2

Mrs Abe's lunch proved a prelude to a new life in Tokyo. I was learning the language and even a few halting sentences helped thrust me into the city. I had also met someone very different from Mrs Abe. Midori Kitagata with her long legs and mini skirts typified many young women in the Tokyo of the late 1980s. She worked, wore too much make-up and boasted a foreign lover. She went to a gym, got drunk when she wanted and lived with the feverish energy of a near anorexic. She was also warm and clever. Her apparent lack of Japanese reserve and her directness were initially most beguiling. Here, I thought, was the modern woman who would change Japanese society. We would spend many wild times together; but she never somehow became a close friend. By contrast, my best friend who I met at the same time as Midori and who in the end became the godmother of my son, displayed a formality typical of the Japanese which made her harder to get to know. But she possessed an inner strength and self-knowledge that Midori neither sought nor even felt necessary.

Midori had been married to a Japanese until he caught her spending three afternoons a week with Charlie, a twenty-six year old English broker five years her junior. The husband insisted Charlie pay him a large sum as compensation. After that, as far as he was concerned, Midori belonged to the foreigner. They lived together uneasily. 'I liked Charlie much better when I only saw him in the afternoon,' she complained.

Midori and I became friends when Charlie thought she had tried to commit suicide. Late one evening Charlie telephoned me from Manila. He had gone to the Philippines with half a dozen colleagues from work. On her own in Tokyo Midori had threatened to kill herself. 'I can't understand why,' he said in exasperation. It seemed plain enough. Midori had left her husband for a lover who was now enjoying himself in the sex capital of Asia. 'I am sure it's just hysterics,' he added. I said that I hardly knew Midori. Surely he could telephone one of her Japanese girl friends? 'I have,' he replied. 'They don't want to get involved.' Reluctantly I got dressed and bicycled over to the block of Western-style flats especially built for foreigners and the very rich where Midori lived with Charlie.

I rang up from the lobby. When Midori failed to answer, I went in search of a policeman. Every neighbourhood in Tokyo possesses its *koban* or police box. I found the nearest and walked in. A policeman in grey uniform sat behind a metal desk. On the wall hung blurred photographs of Japanese terrorists. The policeman and I looked at each other. My Japanese could not cope with such subjects as suicide, death or even a simple request like 'please break down my friend's door'. In China I had employed mime to great effect. The Japanese had not so far appreciated my efforts. They thought I was making fun of them. The image of an expiring Midori resolved me to try again.

I pointed to Midori's apartment block, drew my finger across my throat, grunted, rolled my head to one side and let my tongue loll out. I opened my eyes to see the result. The policeman was gripping his desk and staring at me. I repeated my performance this time with groans. The policeman scrambled through a directory and reached for his telephone. He obviously thought I was in dire need of an ambulance. I shook my head vigorously then attempted a sane and reassuring smile. I stood up, opened the door of the *koban*, stepped out and collapsed on to the pavement trying to give the impression of falling from a great height. I did this two or three times. The policeman got up and closed the door. The draught was making him cold, he explained.

We looked at each other again. I remembered that methods of suicide vary from country to country. Obviously I had failed to hit on one that he recognized. Something quintessentially Japanese was called for. I took off my coat and sat cross-legged on the floor of the *koban*. Slowly I tied my scarf around my head before staring sternly in front of me. I then reached for an imaginary sword, held it up, breathed deeply and plunged it into my stomach. The policeman watched intently. I grunted, paused then dragged the sword sideways and upwards until it reached my heart. Slowly I let my head fall forwards. The policeman nodded, much moved at this impromptu performance of ritual disembowelment. This time when I said 'friend' and pointed to the apartment block, he followed me out.

The policeman found the doorman and together we took the lift to Midori's apartment. We ran down the corridor and hammered on the door. After some time Midori opened it. 'I wouldn't kill myself over Charlie,' she exclaimed. 'I just took a sleeping pill.' Embarrassed and relieved, I lost my temper. The policeman and the doorman, deciding that the vision of Midori in a 'Cuti-doll' nightdress more than made up for any inconvenience, prepared to depart. 'Next time just do it,' I went on. 'You didn't mention that your friend is a TV star,' murmured the policeman. 'She's not,' I snapped. Like all of his foreign friends, I assumed that Midori was supported by Charlie. 'I enjoyed your last show very much,' said the policeman. Midori simpered and replied that it was nothing really, 'certainly beneath an intelligent superintendent's notice'. 'What show?' I interrupted, exasperated at the policeman's pleasure in this sudden promotion.

The policeman explained that the weekly programme showed Midori visiting a well-known Japanese beauty spot. She would discuss its history, chat to a local craftsman or two and sample local delicacies. Last week she had tried an *onsen* in Tohoku, added the policeman with an appreciative look. I stared at Midori in amazement. She never talked about her career. She had never even mentioned that she had one. I wondered if Charlie knew. 'Such a small thing,' said Midori as she autographed the police-

33

man's notebook. 'Nothing compared to your writing,' she added before leading me back into the apartment.

The policeman's admiration failed to hide the fact that Midori did not feel at ease in Japanese society. Divorce, a career, a foreign lover and her age set her apart. She had eschewed the traditional role of wife and mother only to find that Japanese society could provide no other for her to play. Displaced in her own country, she looked to foreigners for company and an identity. This had led to further confusion. She had chosen Charlie because he was a Westerner. She assumed he must offer the freedom of independence associated by Japanese with the West. He had chosen her because she was Japanese and represented to him the bewitching docility of the Oriental woman. With such expectations their affair had inevitably faltered.

I returned to find Nida, our Filipina maid, waiting up for news. Nida worked for us due to a quirk in Japanese immigration law. The Japanese government allowed foreigners to employ Filipina maids. Japanese women married to foreign men were also permitted this luxury but not foreign women married to Japanese men. It is typical of Japan that it was the husband's rather than the wife's nationality which counts with the authorities even in domestic affairs. The husband dictates the character of the household. Japanese husbands are assumed to want their wives at home. Such wives have no need of a maid. The regulations covering the employment of Filipinas proved equally odd. The Japanese government saw nothing wrong in allowing gangsters to import Filipina girls for the sex industry or farmers acquiring them as mail-order brides. They drew the line, however, at women employing the same girls as domestic help. Japanese housewives have to use Japanese maids who charge twice as much (about £2000 a month) and do half the amount of work with a great deal of fuss. We tried a Japanese cleaner once. The amount of hair in the bath so flummoxed her that she never came again.

Nida was short and plump with a coy air that inflamed the elderly carpenter who turned up at our house the next morning.

He had come to hang our paintings. He stared in astonishment at the quantity. He had a wispy beard, a muscular body and resembled a sage on a Japanese scroll. 'Why do you want to hang them all up?' he asked. I explained that we liked having pictures on our walls. 'But so many!' He shook his head. 'In Japan we display one beautiful thing at a time which we change according to the season.' I said that I hardly expected him to return every few months to rearrange my pictures. The carpenter glanced at the kitchen door behind which he could hear Nida humming. It was exactly what he had hoped.

Nida was thirty-five and had lived in Japan for seven years. She had a husband and two children in Manila whom she saw for a month once a year. She had left the children when they were nine and eighteen months old. The state of her country and the high wages paid in Japan had forced her to take this step. Her salary put her in the top 3 per cent of earners in the Philippines. It meant that she could afford to build a house for herself and her parents, pay for private education for her children and employ a maid to take care of the household in her absence. In Manila, Filippinas who worked in Japan were renowned for their wealth. So afraid became Nida's husband of kidnapping that he did not let her walk to the local shop without an escort of himself and her brothers. She only wore jewellery at home. On the street she shuffled about in slippers and an apron.

I went into the kitchen. 'Why don't you offer him a cup of coffee?' I asked. 'That old man!' said Nida indignantly. 'He's only after one thing.' I pointed out that he might give her a good time. Nida hit the kitchen table with her duster. 'My husband would go crazy!' she said with a shiver of satisfaction. She lived, we both knew, a nun-like existence. During the week she stayed with us. She spent the weekends with her two sisters and a sister-in-law all of whom were maids. The sister-in-law reported back to Nida's husband any misbehaviour. This included such innocuous activities as a visit to the bowling alley on the American air force base. The women never went to restaurants or out to a film. Everything cost money and they were there to save. Occasionally, as a big

35

treat, they ate at McDonalds. In Manila the four husbands looked after the children, sat about in bars and had affairs. They declined to work.

At lunchtime Mrs Abe came around with a picnic for the carpenter. She had assumed that I would offer him nothing.

As a reward for rescuing her, Midori suggested we go on a girls' night out. I had feared that her suicide attempt would estrange us. I had embarrassed her and placed her under an obligation. Japanese keep a careful account of favours received. Equally they do everything possible to avoid owing them in the first place. Japanese friends squirmed if my husband paid the restaurant bill or refused outright the most trivial offer of help, as when I suggested posting some letters for Mrs Abe. Midori proved the exception. She explained, 'When Charlie thought that I may have hurt myself, he first rang an old Japanese friend of mine. She was very angry, "If she mixes with foreigners and gets into a mess, she can't then turn to me," was her response. Then he rang you and you came.'

No one enjoys living in Tokyo until they discover Tokyo nightlife. Dusk transforms the city and its inhabitants. Neon lights announcing clubs, restaurants, love hotels and discotheques bloom across every building. Streets are crowded on even the coldest night until two or three in the morning. The regimented Japanese become suddenly spontaneous. At night, all things are permitted. Shame and duty are left at home or in the office. Tokyoites get drunk, seek adventure and create an atmosphere electric with possibility. Into this Midori and I threw ourselves.

When I first arrived in Tokyo, the city was bursting with money and confidence. Like Paris at the end of the nineteenth century, Shanghai before the Second World War and New York thirty years ago, Tokyo in the 1980s proved the stuff of legend. Tokyoites were eccentric, pleasure seeking and amoral. They would spend billions on a painting, millions to plant a garden and thousands merely to sit next to a pretty girl. Tokyoites pursued vice with enthusiasm and imagination. Skyscrapers offered floor after floor of hostess bars and nightclubs with everything from Rastafarian bands to Japanese transvestites, from knickerless waitresses whose skirts flew up when a touch of a customer's button released jets of hot air from the floor, to the most intricate displays of sado-masochism. Drunks were treated with indulgence. Couples, queuing up for a two-hour slot at a love hotel, enjoyed sex without a Western sense of shame. Tokyo's nightlife was as diverse and bizarre as anything on offer in New York. It was also completely safe. I could bicycle from nightclub to floor show, entering male preserves with impunity. Women had nothing to fear but the occasional office worker vomiting over them at a street corner. Even so we got more than we bargained for.

We started in a transvestite bar. A man in a purple kimono greeted us. He had a moustache and wore mascara. 'Fun, fun, fun,' he said encouragingly then sat us at a table with a gorgeous creature in stockings and suspenders. Japanese transvestites behave just like hostesses in conventional bars. They titter behind their fingers and feed you peanuts. Some had pinned up their hair in elaborate rolls. Others preferred wigs which concealed short back and sides. 'He's a railway clerk during the day,' said our host in the purple kimono.

The floor show began. 'They can't be men,' I said as diamante tops slipped off and feather boas undulated over only the briefest of G-strings. Midori admired their bosoms. 'We get them in Singapore,' said the man in the purple kimono. 'They have a marvellous op for £5000. Of course they also do the OTHER operation. That costs £20,000 and there are complications . . .' He and the gorgeous creature discussed which of the dancers in the floor show had suffered these. Just then a group of Old Etonians arrived. 'Do they come here often?' I asked the man in the purple kimono. 'Our best customers,' he declared. 'I will die if they see me,' I said. Midori who had the Japanese matter-of-fact approach to sex could not understand my embarrassment. 'You Westerners talk about sex all the time yet have so many hang-ups. We Japanese don't talk about it, we just do it!'

The Old Etonians appeared unabashed. 'It's tame compared to

37

what Tokyo *can* offer,' they said, ordering us a drink. One recalled a show held in an apartment where guests came by invitation only to watch a girl do unspeakable things with household appliances. Some of the older men had brought magnifying glasses. When it was all over the *mama-san* (the woman in charge) had approached him. 'You are our first foreigner,' she said and asked him to dinner. He had found himself seated next to the star of the evening now wearing a suit and blouse. She was paid £250 and performed once a week. By day she worked as a computer analyst. Why did she do it, he had asked. She enjoyed it, she explained simply.

The Etonians directed us to a pink skyscraper nearby. 'There's a bar or club on every floor,' they said. We started at the top and worked down. In the lift Japanese girls wearing lacy gloves and flouncy mini skirts giggled at us. Two floors of nightclubs gave way to a traditional restaurant complete with tatami mats and shoji screens. The next floor revealed an Indian restaurant, the last, a piano bar which we chose.

The *mama-san* was an attractive woman in her forties. A former lover had paid to set her up as a 'goodbye' present. Like many Tokyo bars, it had been expensively decorated. An enormous vase of lilies stood on the piano. Behind the counter rows of whisky bottles, each bearing a man's name, took up two shelves. These belonged to the regular customers.

Two Japanese men offered us whisky from their bottle. They wore Italian suits, James Dean hair styles and asked if we liked rock concerts. An American entered the bar. 'I hate tall foreigners,' said one of the Japanese. Overcome by the glamour of our drinking companions, we agreed that tall men had nothing to offer. After this we got on splendidly until the Japanese discovered I had a child. 'Why are you here?' they exclaimed in horror. They too had wives and families but their wives stayed at home with the babies. It was my turn for astonishment. Fathers, I said, did not usually wear hair gel or cruise nightclubs. Mutually disillusioned, we parted.

Outside we rejoined the crowds of Japanese. Red-faced salary men, their ties now loosened, hostesses on their way to a new bar, adolescents in black leather, their hair dyed peroxide blond, heavily made up matrons in kimono, all jostled and joked down the street. Gangsters cruised alongside in black Mercedes with tinted windows. At the corner an old man sold hot, sweet potatoes from a cart. From time to time he picked up a megaphone and burst into song. On the edge of the pavement an elderly couple had set up a booth. Behind the flaps, in a space the size of a kitchen table, five or six people had sat down to warm themselves at a kerosene heater and eat noodles.

Half-way down the street we went to investigate the reggae music drifting from an open door. The club had walls of bare brick and lockers in which patrons were advised to leave their belongings. 'Just like London,' I said nostalgically. The club brought a new band from Jamaica every three months. They attracted an eclectic audience. Apart from two young Japanese each wearing one earring, we danced with the black leader of an Australian car trade union, ('I did not know there were any blacks in Australia,' said Midori) and the cook from the Ethiopian embassy. At four in the morning we found ourselves sitting on the pavement learning Rastafarian vocabulary from one of the band. A fat and unhappy black American joined us. When he first came to Tokyo he was thin and pursued. 'I could not walk ten yards down the street without some Japanese girl picking me up.' Eventually he fell for an older woman. She was beautiful and drove a Porsche. Night after night she took him to a different love hotel with bedrooms more extraordinary than the last. He recalled one split-level room with the bed on the upper level from which ran two slides down into a small pool where lovers could meet with a splash. Another was planted with real flowers, allowing the couple to make love on bare earth. 'But that gave me hayfever,' he said regretfully.

His favourite room boasted a railway track and a train in which he sat and chugged around the bed. 'It even had a whistle,' he recalled. One evening his lover said she was sorry but they could not meet again. Her son had to pass an exam. For the next year she had to spend her nights overseeing his studies. 'I still don't

39

understand,' he said. 'Nothing has gone right since,' and he put his head in his hands.

When we left we passed a group of Japanese outside a station waiting for the last train. Some had already begun to prepare themselves for the suburbs, peeling off lacy gloves and smoothing down wild hair. 'They'll be in school uniforms tomorrow,' said Midori. I unlocked my bicycle and pedalled home to my husband.

Midori had given me a glimpse of the *mizu shobai*, the pleasures of the 'floating world' which had characterized old Tokyo. Since the turn of the seventeenth century, the rulers of the country's military capital had set aside an area named Yoshiwara specifically for brothels. Prostitution was banned elsewhere in the city. Fifty years later they moved Yoshiwara north to the then paddy fields of Asakusa. Patrons took a boat up the Sumida river. After landing they crossed a drawbridge called the Bridge of Black Teeth (married women and courtesans traditionally blackened their teeth), paused to buy a straw hat in order to conceal their identity, passed through Omon, the Great Gate, and threw themselves into the wild festivities of the district.

At night rows of paper lanterns lit up the area. Women in kimono with necks and faces painted white took their places in wooden cages set along the pavements. Merchants, samurai, writers, actors and painters mingled in the crowds moving from house to house. They had come not only for sex but also for entertainment and a holiday from an over-regulated society. The Yoshiwara offered an alternative. The high-class courtesans set the fashion in speech, manners and dress. Prints, novels and kabuki plays celebrated their lives and the atmosphere they created. Above all the Yoshiwara was a place to let go. When a man received a windfall or committed a crime he made for the district and stayed until his money ran out.

The prostitutes, of course, had less fun. They were sold as children and kept prisoner behind the Great Gate. Not until 1900 were they permitted to come and go as they pleased. With always more girls available from the countryside, they were treated as expendable items. When they died, and the mortality rate was high, they were thrown into a communal grave at Jokanji temple. The temple register records the average age of the 11,000 girls buried there as twenty-two. The place became known as Nageko-midera, the Dump Temple.

The Yoshiwara was finally abolished in 1959 but its promise of an alternative existence still permeates Tokyo nightlife. Foreigners find it especially attractive. In comparison to ordinary Japanese, its inhabitants appear dashing and eccentric, as I discovered when I met a Japanese gangster.

It began when I was lost, as usual, and studying my map. A Japanese man in black leather caught my eye and winked. The Japanese gangster is as ubiquitous as the crows which infest the city. Top *yakuza* befriend the heads of Japanese securities companies and former prime ministers. The well off monopolize prostitution and gambling while the small time lend money, collect debts and run street festivals. At every level blackmail and extortion comes as naturally as defecation. Like Tokyo's crows, once they choose your car roof, nothing will shift them. So I should not have winked back or asked for directions.

The young man, with a James Dean hair cut and sunglasses, glanced over my shoulder. 'A little far,' he said in abrupt and guttural Japanese. I was intrigued. Japanese men usually avoid Western women and maps fluster the most competent. Instead the man mounted my bicycle and pointed behind him, 'Sit!' he commanded. Hesitantly, I perched sideways, my handbag balanced on my knee. We set off at a wobble, he in black leather, me in a business suit, down the middle of a four-lane highway. Drivers slowed to gape at us. A truck swerved to avoid us. 'I am Yuno,' stated my companion, ignoring the line of cars now crawling behind us. He seemed the antithesis of the Japanese salary man and the Tokyo I knew. Was he, I wondered, a designer? Yuno snorted. 'I am a professional gambler,' he informed me. In Japan professional gamblers are usually members of criminal syndicates. The term for gangster, *yakuza*, in fact stands for 'eight-nine-three', the losing combination of a popular card game. Yuno,

41

the son of divorced parents, had started playing when he was eight. By twelve he was gambling against grown men. 'Now I am twenty-nine and pretty strong.' I gave him my telephone number. He had, after all, got me to my appointment on time.

Yuno rang me from a mahjong parlour on his portable phone. It was two in the morning. 'Say something to bring me luck,' he commanded. I heard the click of mahjong tiles. 'Have you won?' I asked. 'No,' he replied and cut the connection.

It took a month to persuade him to take me gambling. 'Very dangerous,' he said. 'Not for foreigners and certainly not for women.' Finally he picked me up in a black convertible Corvette. He wore a pink, crêpe de Chine shirt, a jacket of lime silk and a suntan. 'First day of spring,' he announced in explanation. One night's winnings had paid for the car. He spoke about that night often. Its memory had obliterated all subsequent losses. Instead of dinner – 'I never eat before I gamble. It makes me sleepy' – we drank coffee in a bar owned by a friend passionate about mountain climbing and South African politics. 'Please give me your opinion of Winnie Mandela,' he asked. Yuno had enjoyed a wild adolescence. He 'shot ice [speed] all the time', got into fights and went to prison for a year. 'Just for a fight?' I asked, astonished. 'Well, he nearly killed the man,' explained his friend. Like a soldier displaying his wounds, Yuno showed me his fake front teeth and scarred left eye. He took pills continually for an ulcer. 'But you are not *yakuza*?' I said unable to associate this eccentric and attractive young man with them or, for that matter, his own past. 'Oh no, I am a professional gambler,' said Yuno and took out his wallet for me to admire. 'Made in England,' he explained. I was more interested in the contents, a thick wad of ten thousand yen notes.

Yuno offered to take me out that evening to Kabuki-cho. I returned home bewildered. Kabuki, traditional Japanese theatre form, was hardly the entertainment I had expected from Yuno. I rang Midori. She was shocked. Kabuki-cho was not a theatre but a district so dangerous that most Japanese refused to go there. 'Sex and gambling,' was how she described it.

42

Yuno picked me up at a street corner, his black car gliding up beside me like a curious shark. We set off for Kabuki-cho or 'Exciting City' as Yuno said. Japanese men in a van gave me the thumbs-up signal. Nothing like that had happened when I was with a foreign man. Most Japanese men normally made a point of ignoring me. At the entrance to the car park the attendant stepped in front of Yuno's car and held up two fists, crossed over each other. Yuno flicked his fingers and the man jumped aside. 'He thinks I am *yakuza*,' said Yuno. It was obviously a gangsters' car park. Rows of black Mercedes with tinted windows stretched in every direction. Yuno's car was the only exception.

The streets were narrow and crowded with neon signs. We passed a large and respectable looking tea room. Yuno explained that this was a favourite haunt of *yakuza*, 'Taipei *yakuza*, Chinese *yakuza*, Japanese *yakuza*, every kind.' The previous year a gun fight in the tea room had killed two men. We passed another club called 'Honky Tonk Girls'. Its doorman wore a giant chick costume, the yellow down now matted and dirty. Yuno stopped and pushed open a door unadorned except for a notice in Thai script. 'The Thais own a lot of clubs,' he explained. Three men with the distinctive tight curls or punch perm of *yakuza*, greeted him warmly. Electronic poker machines filled the small room. Yuno studied a chart displaying each machine's wins for the day. Polaroid snaps stuck on the wall showed happy winners with their hands.

Yuno chose one machine, sat down then shook his head and moved to another. Each game cost ¥10,000 (£60). A win translated into extra playing time rather than money. Yuno played ten games. Never, I reflected sadly, had a man spent so much on me in so short a period with so little to show for it. The club appeared popular with prostitutes. One, older than the rest, arranged appointments for the night over a mobile phone. She worked the poker machine angrily as if surprised at loosing. Finally I told Yuno that he had spent enough. Unused to his dates making that particular complaint, Yuno got up and followed me out. At the door the owner took a polaroid of us.

We now visited a mahjong parlour smaller and even shabbier than the poker club with a low ceiling and no windows. A middle-aged waiter with the end of a punch perm took Yuno's jacket and hung it on a coat stand. I was left to manage on my own. The club had the air of a lumber room. Objects appeared dumped anywhere. Apart from three mahjong tables, I counted an electric massage chair, five swivel seats upholstered in red velvet, a pile of chintz cushions, two electronic poker machines, an old fashioned coat stand and a Hoover. Dusty air conditioning units and unused light fittings cluttered up the ceiling. At one end of the room stood a counter behind which a waitress served Japanese tea, coffee and yoghurt drinks.

As in most Japanese establishments, the service more than made up for the surroundings. Yuno called over the waiter and barked an order. The man hurried back and forth to the coat stand, ferrying objects from Yuno's jacket pocket to its owner. Yuno would take the wallet or the handkerchief then change his mind and send it back. Finally the waiter produced Yuno's glasses. Yuno held them up, shook his head and handed them to the waiter who hastily withdrew behind the counter. He returned, his weak, kind face now hopeful, the spectacles washed and gleaming. Yuno put them on and settled down to play. I was told to sit behind him and keep quiet.

Beneath the harsh strip lighting I watched the mahjong with pleasure. Yuno changed places and sat opposite me, his face, as he slipped the tiles back and forth between his fingers, like that of a good and studious schoolboy. At the end of the game the centre of the table opened and the tiles vanished with a slushing sound. The men waited impatiently for a new lot to appear, their fingers flexed like claws on the baize. Yuno told them I was 'intelligent', as if it were an attribute like long legs which glamorized him. My interest amused them.

A professional player dominated each table. One wore a jade green pullover with a wallet in matching green tucked into his back pocket. The other sported a mustard yellow tracksuit and a black jockey cap inscribed, 'It's A Simple Life'. In moments of stress his wife gave him a shiatsu massage. Otherwise she sat on the sofa with a look of admiring patience which must have taken years to perfect. Surprisingly both men displayed the healthy, outdoor complexion of the professional golfer.

A round lasted twenty minutes at the end of which the men had lost or made about £500. Food was ordered, brought in from outside and consumed quickly between games. The waiter then offered toothpicks. After cleaning his teeth, Yuno told the waiter he wanted to play with the man in the black cap. This had obviously happened before with an unhappy result. The waiter looked sick and mumbled something. The reply enraged Yuno. His face instantly transformed, the skin stretching taut, the eyes bulging over bloodshot rims, into that of a small night predator. The room went silent. The waiter backed away, an arm held up, his head lowered for the blow. Then Yuno caught sight of my expression. He paused, 'It's all right, it's safe,' he said finally, his face falling back into place.

A young, fresh-faced waitress came on duty. She approached each table, bowing twice to the players before taking up her place behind the counter. The men ignored her. A commotion in one corner revealed a *yakuza* who had been asleep behind an upturned table. Pushing aside a blanket, he yawned and stretched. The waitress hurried to his side with a cup of tea. He pulled off his jersey and joined a game.

Every hour Yuno looked at me guiltily and asked for a little longer. At three o'clock I said goodbye and walked through Kabuki-cho in search of a taxi. I sauntered behind a lovely tart with a short skirt, long legs and a chain belt over a full bottom. No one bothered us.

I recounted my adventure to Midori expecting her to be amused. Instead she urged me not to see Yuno again. In Japan *yakuza* and gamblers are one and the same. Traditionally *yakuza* used gamblers to get ordinary Japanese in debt and so in thrall to the gangster. 'Once they have something on you, they never let go,' warned Midori. Japanese take every precaution to avoid *yakuza*. Some even refuse to enter *pachinko* parlours because they are *yakuza*-owned. Westerners were no longer immune either, she added. Sons of wealthy *yakuza* joined Western banks because, unlike Japanese companies, they did not perform background checks. We had one friend who had inadvertently employed a *yakuza*. When our friend sacked him for dishonesty, he received a death threat and had to move into a hotel for safety. His Japanese colleagues insisted he pay the man off and give him a good reference. Midori pointed out that I, too, was vulnerable. *Yakuza* seduced foreign models, introduced them to drugs, then passed the girls around their friends before selling them off to the Triads in Hong Kong. She added, 'Once he finds out that your husband works for a bank, he'll try and compromise you. Blackmail is their business. It's in their nature.' I insisted that I felt safe with Yuno. If he had to choose between a mahjong game and a naked girl, he would not hesitate. The girl would lose out every time.

That Friday Mrs Abe visited bearing a bag of manure and a dictionary. We had grown friendly over a miniature plum tree which she had presented to us as a New Year's gift. In January the blossom had appeared like scraps of pink tissue on the branch. I was determined the tree should bloom again the following year. Mrs Abe had shaken her head and sucked her teeth. Foreigners did not understand bonsai, she explained kindly. Even Japanese found them difficult. I stood firm and she now opened the dictionary and drew up a timetable. The bonsai appeared to require a different amount of sun, water and food each week of the year. I looked helplessly at Nida who scowled. She knew who would be doing all the work.

As she was about to leave, Mrs Abe mentioned the true purpose of her visit. She was meeting an artist friend on Saturday afternoon. Would I care to come? Mrs Abe, like Yuno, issued the most tantalizing invitations at the shortest notice. I promised my husband I would only be a few hours and left him in charge of our small daughter.

As we drove through Tokyo's interminable suburbs, Mrs Abe told me about her friend. Mr Sakuma made paper according to traditions dating back a thousand years to the Heian period. Life for the ordinary Japanese had been short and brutish but the court had produced a culture of fabled exquisiteness. The women wore their hair to the ground, dressed in layer upon layer of carefully chosen silks and enjoyed a measure of freedom unique in Japan's history. Despite concealing themselves behind a screen in a man's presence, they owned land, received an education and took lovers. They chose according to the man's poetic ability. A man, hearing rumour of a woman's beauty or charm, sent her a poem. She replied and there followed an exchange. If both found the correspondence satisfying the man came to her house at night, sliding back the outside shoji screen and creeping into her futon where they would see each other face to face for the first time. In the morning he left before the household awoke. This was mere form. Family and servants had heard what had happened through the paper walls. The new lovers then hurried to their brushes to celebrate the night's events in a fresh bout of poetry. 'Mr Sakuma believes that nothing good has happened since,' said Mrs Abe. She assured me that Mr Sakuma was unique and soon to be honoured by the Emperor with the title of 'Living National Treasure'. I imagined a recluse living in a traditional Japanese house surrounded by paddy fields and bamboo groves.

In fact, the Living Natural Treasure inhabited a block of flats overlooking a dual carriageway. We walked down a corridor open to the air and lined with steel doors. I expected the one in front of which we stopped to conceal a prison cell rather than the thick-haired, handsome-eyed Mr Sakuma.

Mrs Abe bowed deeply and we sat down on our best behaviour. The apartment, small with a low ceiling, resembled thousands that litter Tokyo. From the windows a grey cityscape stretched to the horizon. It seemed hardly the view to inspire a specialist in the crafts of the Heian period. Mr Sakuma's wife backed out of a kitchen no bigger than a cupboard with the tea tray. 'What delicious little cakes!' said Mrs Abe patronizingly. In reply Mrs Sakuma said that she too was an artist, a painter in fact, 'So I have little time for cooking.'

Mr Sakuma showed us his work. Fragments of patterned paper, subtly coloured and seamlessly joined, made up each sheet, the whole then speckled in gold and silver. They appeared the only beautiful items in the flat. Paper had not translated easily, it seemed, into a living for the Sakumas.

Mr Sakuma waited until his wife vanished into the kitchen, then leaned forward. 'I want to give you a present in honour of your visit,' he said shyly to Mrs Abe. He had written a poem on a sheet of paper about a dejected lover recalling his mistress during the seasons. The calligraphy was loose, intimate and tender. When I exclaimed at its romantic nature, Mrs Abe looked coy while Mr Sakuma blushed. Mrs Sakuma appeared at the kitchen door and glared at them both.

It seemed the moment to depart but as we rose to our feet Mr Sakuma announced he owned another home which he pressed us now to visit. Mrs Abe accepted this unexpected invitation with alacrity. Mrs Sakuma looked enigmatic.

We drove for ten minutes to a tree-lined suburb. Mrs Abe appeared taken aback. She glanced at Mr Sakuma, 'So tranquil!' she breathed. She was even more startled by the house in front of which we drew up. Built in Japanese style, it was obviously new and three times the size of her own. Mrs Sakuma gave her rival a triumphant look and led us inside. Paper paid better, after all, than banking.

The house boasted a large tatami room in which Mr Sakuma stored rolls of parchment lined with brocade. Very expensive, these had proved popular with his patrons. The rest of the house was Westernized with a big, airy kitchen. I asked why he kept the apartment. He looked embarrassed not wishing to admit the usefulness of being both a successful craftsman and a poor artist. Finally he said, 'Some people are more comfortable there.'

It was now three o'clock in the afternoon. 'What about lunch?' asked Mr Sakuma. A few days earlier the future Living National Treasure had returned from exhibiting in Rome. He had brought back Italian olives and salami which he served us with a tomato salad and basil grown in the garden. He presented the food on gold-rimmed plates which he had designed himself. He had in fact designed a whole dinner service; 'You can buy it at Harrods,' he assured me. 'Fancy a great artist cooking for us and such good food too!' enthused Mrs Abe. Mrs Sakuma sat silent and smug. I imagined Yuno and thousands of other Japanese grabbing lunch in a fast-food restaurant. We seemed not quite in the Heian period but certainly a world away from my preconceptions. Mrs Sakuma unbent and became quite jolly. Twice I rang my husband to apologize for my absence. 'Just like a good Japanese wife,' teased the future Living National Treasure as he filled my glass with some excellent Italian wine. I arrived home drunk and three hours late.

Yuno called the following week. He had finally left the mahjong parlour at nine in the morning after losing ¥200,000 (£1200). 'I was well up around four o'clock,' he remarked wistfully. I asked why he had not left then. Yuno did not bother to reply. It was a stupid question to ask a gambler. He had fallen asleep in his car until lunchtime. I suggested that we meet in his friend's coffee shop. He agreed with alacrity. Two coffees was about all he could afford.

I found him gossiping with a retired boxer. Yuno had parked outside the coffee shop. An ordinary Japanese would have had his car towed away by now but not Yuno. The police had not touched his. I recalled Midori's troubling questions. A warm, wet wind had begun to blow. Yuno hesitated then invited me to go gambling again.

In the car I asked if he ever had time for girlfriends. Yuno admitted that he took one day off a week from gambling. 'Of course I want a girlfriend very much but no Japanese girl will go with me.' I asked why but he shook his head and laughed. He had had an Israeli girlfriend who had impressed him with her stories of being a soldier in the Israeli army but she had returned home. We drove for a short time in silence. Then he said, 'What I really want is not a girlfriend but a baby.'

We parked outside a block of flats in a respectable area of town. Yuno was nervous. 'We are going to meet very dangerous men,' he said. I was instructed to sit behind him, not to say a word and to pretend to be his girlfriend. Shortly afterwards I found myself in a room with ten Japanese gangsters.

The room itself boasted a low ceiling with strip lighting and no furniture but a plastic sofa on which I perched. The gangsters had punch perms or crew cuts. Most wore tracksuits. They squatted on the tatami or stood about making a point of not looking at me. There were no other women. Apprentice *yakuza* took coats, made tea or proffered a kitchen sieve full of sweets. They behaved as deferentially as any Japanese salary man to his section head. The boss, an intelligent man in his early forties, asked me if I enjoyed gambling. 'Money's no problem here,' he said, handing Yuno a packet. Above his head hung photographs of karate experts and an oil painting of a roaring tiger. Through the doorway I glimpsed longjohns pegged up to dry. These men were also celebrating the first day of spring but rather differently from Yuno.

Local street traders now arrived and joined the gangsters around a sheet taped on to the tatami. They played *tehon biki*, a Japanese form of liar dice. Yuno dealt first. He shuffled the cards behind his back then slapped them down beneath a cloth. The men bet on which card lay uppermost. It was not a difficult game but, posing in his sunglasses, his pink shirt falling open, Yuno kept on asking questions and getting things wrong like a spoilt and beautiful woman. 'My family,' he said, effusively and then, nodding towards the boss, 'my elder brother.'

A small Japanese squatted down next to me. Behind him towered his companion, a massive *yakuza* in a yellow tracksuit. At the sight of this couple the street traders went quiet and concentrated on their bets. I wish I could have done the same. The small man spat out a command. Immediately an apprentice *yakuza* appeared with an orange juice. The massive *yakuza* grunted a dismissal. The small man now made himself comfortable. As he did so his jeans rucked up to reveal suspenders holding up his socks. Between sock and suspender the tattoo of a red dragon's tail thrashed against peonies on one leg and purple clouds on the other before disappearing upwards. Tattoos are the stigmata of the dedicated *yakuza*. In an agonizing process lasting six months the entire body is covered. Yuno pushed back his sleeve to reveal a single bleeding heart. 'American style,' he explained, 'and so not painful at all.' The small man was more interested in the size of my feet. He edged one of his next to my much larger foot then withdrew it quickly, in a huff.

He cheered up as Yuno lost more and more money to him. 'I'll win it back,' confided Yuno. The massive *yakuza* stared at us then rubbed his punch perm reflectively. I pressed Yuno to leave. He looked vague. 'Just a little longer,' he murmured. Reluctantly I stood up and, on Yuno's instructions, bowed to elder brother. At the door Yuno handed me thirty thousand yen. 'From elder brother. Now you are family friend too, neh?' he said and pushed me out before I could protest.

I did not hear from Yuno again. When I rang his portable phone, a recorded message in a prissy lady's voice announced the owner had gone for a short walk. After a month I gave up trying.

'Have you seen my black magic woman?' asked the small French man. Pierre lived with Annunciation, a Jamaican whose beauty and presence ensured a career as a catwalk model despite being over forty. She was also the only woman looking good at the 'cross dressing' party that night. The rest of us stood morosely around the edge of the room in our husband's suits and ties.

In the centre cavorted the men, transformed by mini skirts, wigs and false eyelashes. The most lovely was Charlie, wearing an elegant sequinned dress of Midori's and a wig of auburn hair curling down to his waist. A crowd of young brokers surrounded him. 'Darling', or 'You bitch', they squealed with equal rapture. All exuded confidence for they were young men with a real sense of privilege. Charlie was fairly typical. The son of a retired British diplomat, he had been to public school and enjoyed an international background. Whereas most of his contemporaries shrank from working in a place as alien as Japan, Charlie looked with relief on the chance to escape London. As he said, 'I can't live in a city where there's nowhere to eat breakfast at four in the morning.'

Japan had increased his self-confidence. Charlie was earning more money at twenty-five than his father at the height of a civil-service career. 'I'm sending my parents a couple of First Class tickets so they can visit me,' he had remarked carelessly. He exuded a barely suppressed exhilaration which overspilled on occasions like tonight. He found himself in an extraordinary place during a period of extraordinary growth. He recalled England dimly and with pity. 'My friends have become so parochial,' he said after one trip back. 'They barely know France exists, much less Tokyo.' Now he turned and caught sight of himself in the mirror. He paused, startled at the cheek bones and elegant legs. Even as a woman, he was better than many of the real thing.

Annunciation picked on this moment of self-satisfaction to attack him from behind with a teddy bear. Before Charlie could protest, she had whipped up his skirts and slipped the bear over his stomach. 'A pregnant Charlie!' she exclaimed with delight. Midori watched Charlie prance around from friend to friend receiving congratulations and pats. She was sitting on one side talking to another Japanese girl, her figure entirely hidden by one of Charlie's golfing jerseys. Unlike our evenings together, she wore no make up. 'Charlie prefers me this way,' she explained.

Later Annunciation lit mosquito coils and we moved outside into her small, overgrown garden. Midori sat in Charlie's arms on an old sofa. Her happiness at his attention softened her face and made her look very young. Charlie was discussing his Japanese colleagues with an Indian friend who had grown up in Yokohama and spoke fluent Japanese. Charlie was complaining, 'Japanese don't have any concept of friendship. Friends are merely the people they work with. When they change jobs they change friends.' Midori looked pained as she always did when he criticized Japan, but said nothing. Charlie saw her expression and lifted up a handful of her hair. 'Who wants Japanese men?' he asked. 'Who's interested in them when there are Japanese women,' and he buried his face in her hair and stroked her skin.

Two other young brokers came outside. Charlie had enjoyed an adventure the night before and they wanted to hear about it. He leaned forward, confident of telling a good story. 'After a great deal of drink and drugs,' he started, 'I found myself at two in the morning in a cab on my way home with only ¥800 in my pocket.' When the metre hit that amount, he stopped the cab, got out and contemplated the long walk home. Suddenly he saw a bicycle chained to a lamppost. He paused only a moment before doing something he would never have considered in England. He picked up a can and was breaking the lock when someone grabbed his shoulder, '*Gaijin-san*! Mr Foreigner!' said a severe voice. Hastily Charlie stood up and found himself facing an elderly Japanese policeman. He explained it was his friend's bike. The policeman looked unconvinced. A second fat policeman pedalled up on his bicycle. Both began to suck their teeth and shake their heads. Charlie recalled, 'My boss was in town, my assistant was on holiday and I had to be in work at 7 a.m. I looked at the two policemen, one fat and one old and thought, I can get out of here, so I ran for it.'

As he sprinted down the road, congratulating himself, he heard the wail of a police car. 'Shit!' he thought and turned into a side street. When the car followed he decided to lose it amongst the mesh of alleyways that lie behind Tokyo's main roads but found himself in a dead end. He opened a front door and crouched in the hall of a small Japanese house. The police car pulled up. Charlie knocked over a pile of shoe boxes which aroused a middle-aged woman who appeared in pyjamas. She saw Charlie and screamed. 'Come out foreigner!' wailed the policeman over his megaphone. Sheepishly Charlie stepped from the front door with his hands up. The housewife followed yelling and jabbing his back and ribs. Caught between the irate woman and the furious policeman, Charlie pretended ignorance of Japanese. The policemen grabbed him by the shoulders and threw him into the car. The housewife watched with satisfaction as they beat him up. At the police station they booked him for stealing a bicycle, evading arrest and breaking and entering.

Charlie paused to rearrange Midori on his lap. 'They had left me in a cell, contemplating deportation and the end of my career when in walked the head of the station.' The man wore his hair slicked back and was smoking a cigarette. Charlie and he looked each other over in silence. Charlie was intensely interested in people's motivations. Whether discussing literature with me or blow jobs with a Japanese colleague, he enjoyed an uncanny ability to empathize and win people to his side. It was what made him such a successful salesman. Sometimes I wondered who was the real Charlie, so much did he take his colouring from other people. On his own I imagined him washed out almost to a shadow. Under pressure, however, he lit up like a Christmas tree.

He hesitated, then putting aside the pretence of knowing no Japanese, sprung to his feet and erupted into deep bows and profusions of apologies. 'Maybe I made a mistake, maybe the bike did not belong to my friend,' he finally conceded. The superintendent's face softened infinitesimally. Charlie did not let up for a moment. '*Gaijin* card!' interrupted the policeman. Charlie faltered. By law every foreigner must have a card bearing his photograph and finger print (this applies even to foreigners who have lived in Japan for two or three generations) which has to be carried at all times. Charlie admitted he had left his at home. 'We'll go to your apartment to get your passport and *gaijin* card,' said the superintendent. 'Good, I thought, at least I'm getting a ride home,' said the ever-optimistic Charlie. They set off in a car with both the old and the fat policemen.

On the way the superintendent asked Charlie what sports he liked. 'Surfing,' replied Charlie. The superintendent said that was his favourite too. He had surfed since highschool and in fact had just come back from a surfing holiday in South Africa. When they arrived at the apartment, Charlie got out his surfing photographs. He and the superintendent settled down to look at them on the balcony with a couple of beers. 'All this time the policemen who had beaten me up had to wait outside in the stuffy corridor,' recalled Charlie with satisfaction. After an agreeable hour or so the superintendent stood up and shook Charlie's hand. He said, 'Don't do that again, *gaijin-san*. But if you want to go out drinking, just give me a call.'

We all applauded, agreeing that only in Japan could that happen. The eccentric behaviour of the superintendent summed up much of the pleasure of life in Tokyo. We put down Charlie's escape to his charm but there was something else. Foreigners like us inhabited a privileged position. In a society where everyone was acutely aware of their responsibilities, we had none. We were required to give nothing; we only took.

Later that evening half a dozen of us ended up in a nightclub where much to everyone's interest and with Annunciation and Midori as midwives, Charlie gave birth to the teddy bear.

3

My experience with Yuno made me determined to improve my Japanese. Learning the language, like finding one's way in Tokyo, is a series of baffling experiences leading to an initiation which proves no initiation at all. Foreign grammar books present Japanese as a puzzle that with a bit of effort fits perfectly together. Spoken Japanese is a different story. It traps, evades and obfuscates the would-be speaker. Foreigners like myself were armed by their teachers with a form rarely used by Japanese themselves because it is innocuous and neutral. Every other form proves explosive in the hands of the unwary. It leads the foreigner to the point where language and culture connect, the moment when a foreigner starts thinking like a Japanese and seeing himself in relation to others as a Japanese does.

That moment came for me when I learnt how to describe receiving a favour. In England, 'Can you water my plants while I am on holiday?' is a question which carries no heavy social implication. In Japan it was linguistic dynamite and required a week's preparation before I could address it to my formidable neighbour, Mrs Abe. First I had to categorize both of us. My position *vis à vis* the person doing me the favour dictated which verb I employed to make my request. Obviously Mrs Abe was not my inferior nor an old friend. We were not part of the same group, did not belong to the same family, attend the same university or work in the same office. Therefore I had to employ a formal verb, but exactly how formal? She considered herself my superior but she was also my neighbour. If my language proved too elevated she would find it just as insulting as if I failed to show respect. The exercise forced me to look at my relationship with Japanese society in a new way. It was the moment when I realized that I was absorbing more than just language.

The exercise also taught me that Japanese note even the most trivial obligation linguistically. I had finally persuaded Mrs Abe to let me pick up some dry cleaning for her. When another neighbour asked if she had collected it, Mrs Abe's reply revealed the importance she attached to this simple transaction. To her it marked a new stage in our relationship. She said, 'No, I received the picking up of the dry cleaning.' In other words, 'No, I did not do it. Harriet did me a favour and picked it up for me.' Her acceptance of my help showed, as the neighbour immediately understood, that Mrs Abe liked me. She now felt obliged to do me a good turn and the obligation to see me again was no longer onerous to her. Somewhere, I supposed, in the minutiae of future transactions glimmered the start of a friendship.

Japanese is also a language of apartheid. Sound, syntax and vocabulary consign people to rigid categories. I learnt a different Japanese from my husband and even from my small daughter who had just started Japanese nursery school. The polite language expected from women with its sliding syllables forced me talk in a soft, breathless voice. My husband's Japanese proved quite the opposite: his voice dropped and the sentences scattered out in harsh bursts like machine-gun fire. Syntax and vocabulary altered radically depending on the speaker. In the same sentence uttered by Mrs Abe and Yuno, 70 per cent of the words would have been different. It made Japanese even harder to comprehend than to speak. I knew five ways to ask the age of a child; but it only took a lorry driver to question me in a casual fashion or a shop assistant to employ a flattering term reserved for customers to leave me flummoxed. As a woman I was expected to understand and use polite forms. For months I begged everyone to address me in simple Japanese. After Mrs Abe's circumlocutions, I found Yuno and his *yakuza* friends refreshingly easy to comprehend.

Mrs Abe held that Japanese was the politest language in the world by which she meant that it had numerous polite forms. I replied that English too relied on the conditional to soften requests, the difference being in how it is used. English is much more flexible. The conditional is lavished as much on plumbers as on duchesses. Mrs Abe exhibited horror at this. She used one language for inferiors and another for superiors. Kindliness, gratefulness, a long relationship, none of these caused her to deviate: a plumber was always a plumber. Language merely reflected the hierarchical nature of Japanese society. Power in Japan confers infallibility. There is no call for the powerful to employ the arts of self-effacement used by their counterparts in the West.

The hierarchical nature of the society is responsible for another characteristic of Japanese. It is a language designed to avoid confrontation. Nothing need be said outright. The tone of the voice and the choice of vocabulary conveys it all. It is a language to take cover behind. Communication is a battlefield and Japanese offers scores of ways to avoid a calamitous entanglement. Whenever I started on one of those tentative conversations the history of Japan seemed to press down upon me. I felt myself transported to a social system so rigid and so brutal that as late as the second half of the nineteenth century a samurai had the right by law to test his sword by decapitating a peasant. Vagueness became a necessity and a virtue. The verb at the end of the sentence, for example, allowed the speaker to trim his speech to his listener's reaction. It is quite opposite from the Western concept of language. There the presumption is optimistic. Language is a bridgehead between two people who would otherwise remain isolated. It presumes understanding leads to compassion. In such an atmosphere clarity of expression becomes an intellectual ideal, frankness, its emotional equivalent.

Japanese proved to be frank in a different way. When Midori and I visited a sushi bar we guessed the history of the couple squashed against us by the forms they used to one another. In the office my husband knew if his Japanese colleague was chatting on the telephone to his wife, an old client, one he had just made, a bar girl or a distant relative simply by his choice of words. Japanese teased Charlie because he had picked up his Japanese from Midori. His feminine vocabulary betrayed not only how he had learnt it but even the background of his girlfriend. 'Rather an ordinary girl?' hazarded Mrs Abe who had met Charlie in our house without Midori. She had seen a photograph of Charlie in a glossy, foreign magazine. 'He moves in high society?' she asked, impressed, then added, 'Perhaps he should find himself a better class of girlfriend.' There is nothing subtle about Japanese snobbery, however it is couched.

Japanese, I discovered, is a surprisingly emotional language. In the ninth century, Japan borrowed extensively from Chinese, including the written language. Words of Chinese origin have a similar relation to original Japanese words as English words with a Latin stem do to those with an Anglo Saxon derivation. Japanese newscasters employ Chinese compounds because they carry no emotional weight. On the other hand, original Japanese words resound with feeling. I was on a train with three old Japanese ladies. We had been on an outing together with my daughter in whom they had shown great interest. Finally one explained that all three of them were barren. 'We married at the same time, lived near each other and then could not have children. That is why we are such good friends.' They were fortunate to avoid childbirth, I said in an effort to be cheerful. The old lady shook her head, 'Sabishi desu ne?' 'It's sad, isn't it?' Even to me 'sabishi' carries such powerful connotations of loneliness and misery that I was silent and had to turn away.

The cumulative effect of learning the language was forcing me to behave more and more as a Japanese. The different forms of address required a different tone of voice, even a different way of holding myself. Almost unconsciously I began to assume that all-important armour for a woman in Japan, the respectful attitude. At first I viewed it as a delightful game, a kind of play-acting. Then I realized its value. Japanese reacted immediately when I got it right; suddenly life became easier. Minor officials smiled at me. Shop-keepers picked out the best fruit. Policemen indulged misbehaviour. I began to enjoy Japan. Another side to this country existed; and my Japanese was beginning tantalizingly to reveal it.

How much of a native I had become Japan Railways put to the test when they auditioned me for an announcer on their high-speed trains. Recorded announcements are made in both English and Japanese. The Chairman of Japan Railways had taken against the previous recordings made by an American. Only a British accent would do, which meant, in Japan, a British woman's voice. They appointed an agent, an unsavoury middle-aged Japanese in black leather who drove me to the audition.

Tokyo is a city of female voices; from the moment one steps on to the escalator at Narita airport the recorded lisp of a Japanese woman instructs and beguiles. Her vocabulary is distinctive. Everything must be called by a softer, more honorific term that tinkles off the tongue. Not a television set can be heard, a ticket machine used or a lift entered without her high, breathless voice. Its owner one pictures in lacy tights, her hair in bangs, giggling behind her fingers. She wants three things, marriage, babies and a flat in the suburbs. Her vocabulary is as much a part of the tender trap as the lacy tights, it promises hot dinners, docility and the occasional ecstatic moment. This was the voice I now had to emulate.

Ten officials from Japan Railways greeted me at the recording studio. After much bowing and exchanging of name cards they handed me a form to fill in. Was I a graduate, they asked anxiously. The Chairman liked graduates. I told them I had attended Oxford University. This failed to impress. Instead the officials eyed me as one might eye a horse that has learnt to talk. My rival proved small, dark and pretty. Stephanie had not attended university. She was a model. The officials looked her over approvingly. Safely exotic rather than large, blond and freakish like myself, she was the sort of foreigner Japanese prefer.

Japanese salary men, she confided, constantly felt her up in the underground. They avoided standing even close to me.

The officials asked us each to read out an announcement. 'Ladies and gentlemen, welcome to our Shinkansen. . .' boomed my voice over the system. Stephanie issued her greeting with even more authority, but then she had grown up in Hong Kong. I almost expected the officials to fetch her fan or a glass of water. We sat down assuming they would pick one of us and start recording. Instead the Japanese officials remained silent. The technicians fiddled with their instruments. Finally the agent, whom we had both taken against, cleared his throat. There seemed to be a problem. We sounded condescending which was unacceptable to the Japanese public. Japanese liked gentle voices, 'and please smile all the time.'

We took it in turns to try again. I repeated 'Ladies and gentlemen' for an excruciating forty-five minutes. The Japanese were flummoxed by my inability to get it right. Stephanie said, 'We make public announcements differently in England.' I thought briefly of a British Rail announcement, inaudible and apathetic. Finally one official begged me to imagine myself a mother. He then seated the agent opposite me in the recording booth. 'Your child,' he said, patting the agent on the shoulder. The agent crossed a leather-clad leg and screwed up his face into an expression of expectant sympathy. 'Speak the lines as a mother to her child,' everyone urged. Tenderly I listed the stations between Tokyo and Nagoya. A silence ensued. 'Again!' rapped an official. I balked, pointing out the absurdity of an English woman making an English announcement in Japanese style. They stared at me, uncomprehending. 'But this is Japan,' they said. A loss of temper brought insight. 'You want me to sound like a Japanese woman!' I exclaimed. With relief the officials turned to Stephanie. They had always known I would be trouble.

The audition over, the officials handed us each a present of a shaver and an alarm clock. Mistaking the cause of our dissatisfaction, they pointed out that the gifts came from Takashimaiya. 'Tokyo's most expensive store,' they beamed. We had not the heart to ask why the presents were for our husbands and not ourselves. They provided the explanation soon enough. 'Please thank your husbands for allowing you to spare the time,' they added on the final bow.

Stephanie went on to record the announcements over the next two months. The Japan Railways officials presented her with tapes of Japanese women. 'Please listen and practise at home,' they said. The place names gave particular trouble. Hiroshima took an hour to get right. After fifty minutes they asked her to pronounce it, 'Hiloshima'. Stephanie pointed out that foreigners had no trouble pronouncing 'r' and would not understand the substitution. The officials remained unmoved. Never mind if an English person was recording a tape for an English-speaking audience, it still had to be done the Japanese way. 'They could not conceive that another method might exist,' said Stephanie.

The agent also caused trouble. He delayed paying Stephanie the first instalment. She then discovered he was keeping 80 per cent of the money provided by Japan Railways for the project. Japan Railways refused to interfere. Finally she took him to his bank, stood outside and started to scream. She only stopped after he had gone in, withdrawn the money and handed it over.

The recordings continued painfully. 'Please more smile,' repeated the officials. At last she got it right. She explained that the moment came when she exchanged the image of the Japanese public as a wayward child for the audience in the back row of a blue movie theatre. She called it 'Blow Job Talking'. The results were instantaneous. The officials burst into smiles. 'That's it,' they exclaimed. 'That's what we Japanese like to hear!' From then on she had no trouble.

In order to practise my Japanese, I decided to become a hostess. The hostess bar is the fast-food version of the geisha house. It is cheaper, less elaborate, requires no special training and offered me the perfect environment for conversation.

Hostess bars are very popular in Japan. During the boom years of the late 1980s Ginza, the nightclub district for Tokyo's

63

politicians and businessmen, boasted 41,000 bars and 60,000 hostesses. The bars charged from £50 to £500 a head for a modest drink, a bowl of peanuts and a chat or 'charm charge', as the bill stated.

The daughter of an English colonel had given me the idea over Sunday lunch. She worked in a hostess bar three times a week. Her *mama-san*, a woman of about fifty who ran the bar, was proud of her British connections. As well as the colonel's daughter, she employed a black girl from Brixton, a divorcee from Hull and two Sloane Rangers who had run out of money on their way to Australia. The Sloane Rangers had proved excellent at leading the customers in 'Green Grow the Rushes Oh!' Otherwise it was 'hard chat' from seven to midnight. Every night, said the colonel's daughter, clients talked about the same thing: their singing ability and where they had bought their Dunhill lighters. This suited my level of Japanese so I asked what she found irksome about the job. She replied, 'Going to the lavatory. There is only one and I can never go before a client. Sometimes I have to wait fifteen minutes.' When she finished she had to fold the end of the lavatory paper into a neat triangle ready for the next customer. The *mama-san* also insisted that she telephone clients in their office and beg them to visit the club. 'You can imagine what a twit I feel doing that!' Nearly all the customers were married. A weekend of family life, often spent with small children in a one-room flat, made Monday night the busiest evening. Any hostess who did not turn up on Monday lost two nights' pay.

All this sounded very innocuous. Did she really receive no further invitations? 'Oh no,' she paused, 'although sometimes they ask me to go on a weekend's mountain climbing.'

Tokyo's nightlife provided an excellent living for a couple from Newcastle I met on a night out with Midori. The husband worked as a bouncer while his wife earned £100 a night with another £100 in tips as a hostess in one of Ginza's most expensive bars. She explained, 'Foreign hostesses are in demand now. Japanese men think we're exotic. It's fashionable to be international and we are about as international as they will ever get.'

She said Japanese men liked to show off by spending a lot of money on women, 'as if we were cars'. One night a girl burst into tears because she had lost her fur jacket. The next evening a customer arrived with a replacement as a present. Jane admitted she found it difficult explaining her work to her mother. Finally she said, 'It's just like being a barmaid without the bar – I had more trouble from the men in the clubs at home than here.'

She knew of many English girls who had come to Japan for a year then earned so much that they stayed for eight. They lost their looks quickly. 'Its very ageing, smiling all the time,' said Jane. Girls who became prostitutes found the money 'fantastic'. When one girl died while in Tokyo, her parents inherited half a million pounds. She had arrived in Tokyo two years previously as a language student. They thought she was still studying.

I answered a newspaper advertisement seeking foreign hostesses for a Ginza bar. Friends warned, 'All bars are run by *yakuza*. Check their little fingers.' Erring *yakuza* cut off the tip of their little fingers as a sign of loyalty. After my adventures with Yuno I felt equal to dealing with any number of Japanese gangsters.

The interview began badly. I had not had time to change out of clothes more suitable for tea with an elderly Japanese lady. The young man who met me outside Seibu department store, Tokyo's equivalent of Harvey Nichols, wore jeans and a tee-shirt. Both his little fingers proved to be intact. He smiled encouragingly and led me to a basement down a side street. It was dark and so small that one step took me across the dance floor. Over the ceiling spread a giant spider's web made of metal and adorned with huge metallic flies. African drums and the horns of small wild animals hung on the wall. The young man returned, transformed by a black suit into something altogether more sinister. 'Experience?' he snapped. 'None,' I said crisply, then remarked on the ceiling. He got up and left. Other men came to inspect me. My clothes puzzled them and I feared they were not taking me seriously. Finally I said in English, 'Do I have to inform you if a customer arranges to see me after hours?' Silence fell. From across the room, all five feet away, the boss nodded. I was ushered over.

The boss was small and fat and sat behind a large bowl of fruit. This was not eccentricity. Fruit in Tokyo is very expensive and as much of a status symbol as a plate of caviar. Over us loomed his hoods, many with little fingers missing. I took a seat beside a pretty Japanese girl also after the job. No one said anything. I complimented the boss on his club. He did not reply. The Japanese girl stared timidly at the fruit. I was starting on the weather when he picked up the bowl of plums and offered us one. 'So much nicer than English plums,' I said uncertainly. The boss split his plum with his thumbnail and sucked at it with gusto. The juice spurted over his tie, the Japanese girl and me. The Japanese girl looked at her plum then began to peel off the skin in tiny, dainty pieces. I put the plum in my mouth. Another, but more meaningful silence followed. Thoughtfully the hoods watched the mess I made before one passed me a napkin. The Japanese girl now tackled her fruit with neat, dry nips. We both knew who had won. The interview was over.

As I passed Seibu department store on my return I saw an English girl waiting. She wore a low-cut, pink, flouncy dress and vermilion lipstick. Not a girl, I decided, to eat her plums without forethought, and I went home.

Still eager to improve my Japanese, I sought help from Mrs Abe's luncheon club. I had now attended several sessions. Every month one member cooked lunch for the others in her home. Finally my turn arrived. I had no idea what to do. How could I compete, for example, against Mrs Kobayashi who had served iced pond weed gathered from a pond outside her country villa in Izu? My mother who comes from Cape Town where they eat Malay food suggested *bobotie*, a curry with a custard topping. The side dishes of banana, almonds, coconut, raisins and popadums entranced the Japanese ladies, as did my meagre possessions. They examined the china and exclaimed over the sterling silver photograph frames. They expected everything to have a story behind it. Mrs Tashiro studied my sister's paintings. Mrs Kobayashi showed particular interest in some curtains which had been made in England. She got down on her hands and knees to examine the hem. One of the richest women in Japan had never seen interlining before.

Mrs Abe, nervous that her protégé might have let her down, finished lunch in a softened mood. Over coffee I put forward my idea. I wanted to take up charity work and needed information. The ladies exchanged glances. What exactly did I mean, asked Mrs Kobayashi. Charity work would provide me with an opportunity to improve my Japanese, I explained. 'That might be difficult. . .' Mrs Tashiro allowed her voice to trail off suggestively. Mrs Kobayashi nodded in agreement. I stared at them astonished. I had assumed that like their equivalents in London and New York, all three women would be active on various committees. Mrs Abe shook her head. 'I have no contact with charitable organizations of any sort,' she stated. Rather like interlining, it appeared an activity unpractised in Japan.

Mrs Abe explained kindly. 'We have so few social problems compared to your country. We have no need for such kind of thing.' I began to mention the gangs, *burakumin* (the Japanese version of untouchables), amphetamine abuse, the abortion rate and the fact that 40 per cent of Japanese homes are still unconnected to mains drainage then thought better of it. Instead I made my point in a way calculated to appeal to the twin obsessions of certain Japanese, class and history. In English past, I explained, the lady of the manor performed good works. Rich and aristocratic women, here I smiled at my companions, now continued the tradition. Even this failed to bridge the gap between Christian and non-Christian culture. Values I had assumed basic were alien concepts to Mrs Abe and her friends. 'My daughter studies calligraphy,' said Mrs Tashiro helpfully. Mrs Abe explained, 'Japanese of our class spend our time attending cooking or flower arranging classes. That way you will meet the right sort of person and learn good Japanese. We do not indulge', here she wrinkled her nose, 'in "Fun Runs".' She then changed the subject and asked about my coffee pot.

Finally I received help from another group of Japanese ladies with whom I and two English friends regularly lunched. One of them, Mrs Nakamura, who had connections with UNICEF, offered to introduce me to a social worker. We all met in Sumida-ku, Tokyo's equivalent of the East End of London and about an hour from my house on the subway. Tokugawa Ieyasu had reclaimed this marsh during his vast waterworks project in the early years of the seventeenth century. Beyond the moats which protected the homes of his retainers and vassal lords lay the bayfront. On this damp landfill settled the merchants and craftsmen attracted to the expanding city. The district became known as Shitamachi or Low City. Merchants and shopkeepers built two-storied houses along the main streets with earthen walls and tiled roofs. They painted their homes a rich black made from the ash of burnt oyster shells, lime and India ink. Down the back streets lay the slums. They fronted on to alleyways less than a metre wide with an open drain running down the middle. Houses here consisted of a kitchen and a small back room. The lavatory was communal. Many of the old people I met in Shitamachi grew up in these euphemistically named 'long-houses'.

When Japan began to industrialize in the nineteenth century, Sumida-ku's position along the banks of the Sumida river made it an ideal site for factories. From all over the country people moved here looking for work. Hardship produced a unique culture. In this century, natural disasters and war obliterated the area. The Great Kanto earthquake of 1923 devastated 95 per cent of southern Sumida-ku killing 48,000 people. During the Second World War, like the East End, its factories drew the heaviest amount of bombing. From January 1945 to August of the same year 102 American bombing raids destroyed two-thirds of Sumida-ku. The building boom after the war destroyed any remnants of the former Low City.

The distinctive atmosphere of Shitamachi still lives on in its traditions, festivals and cramped, working-class neighbourhoods. At the heart of one of the poorest stands the Kobokan, one of Japan's few private community centres. It was here that the social worker first took me.

We found the Kobokan down a side road surrounded by a

flotsam of tiny houses. It is a sprawling building with walls of cracked cement. A muddy playground stretches behind. A man in his thirties with a shock of thick, springy hair hurled himself out of the door at us. This was Mr Sato, the vice-president of the Kobokan. He bowed and bowed again, talking all the time with great energy. We took off our shoes and put on worn red slippers. A line of volunteer workers all in the same red slippers bowed to us and murmured greeting. I felt more like royalty than the minor helper I hoped to be.

Still talking Mr Sato led us through a series of corridors, rooms and outside passageways which appeared to have spread fungus-like of their own volition. There were people and children everywhere. The Kobokan catered to all age groups from infants of three months to the elderly in their nineties. In the nursery toddlers lay sprawled out on futons fast asleep. Teachers patted wakeful ones on the back or wrote reports. In a vast and shabby gymnasium, 'the largest room in the area', Mr Sato informed us proudly, older children waiting for their parents to pick them up after work stopped playing to stare at me.

The Kobokan was founded in 1919 by Canadian missionaries who wished to emulate the philosophy of Hull House in Chicago which itself drew inspiration from Toynbee Hall in the East End of London. Mr Sato explained with an impassioned expression that this was 'an attitude to people, of loving thy neighbour and living with them'. In the 1920s the area was infamous for its poverty and its prostitutes. Families commonly included ten children. The missionaries provided a nursery and a clinic as well as classes for mothers in hygiene and birth control. The clinic gave many Japanese their first experience of Western medicine. The missionaries appointed a Japanese director in 1929 and the Second World War severed any remaining connections. Their influence, however, still lingered. This had not Westernized the Kobokan, it simply set it apart from anything that I had come across in Japan.

In the centre of the gymnasium a bulky man with a crew cut contemplated a pile of milk cartons. Mr Sato introduced him as the art director. He was in charge of lighting for the rock concert taking place that night in the gymnasium. He seemed much more preoccupied with the milk cartons. He wanted to make a raft from them and float down the Sumida river. 'A rock concert!' I said. In explanation Mr Sato led me to a window, pushed it open and climbed out on to a fire escape. Cautiously I hoisted myself after him. Together we scrambled up to what appeared to be a deserted top floor. 'This is where our young men live,' said Mr Sato proudly.

Mr Sato's young men had grown up in the Kobokan's Children's Home in Karuizawa, a mountain resort three-hours drive from Tokyo. The Home received abused children from the Tokyo metropolitan area. The Japanese government paid for these youngsters to be taken care of until they were eighteen. After that they were on their own. Mr Sato explained, 'Most are not ready for independence so they live here where we can keep an eye on them. This is a sort of half-way house to life.' He also found them jobs locally. He explained that the Kobokan had strong ties to the area. The After School Care programme and the nursery had existed so long that the original participants were now grand-parents. Those who had started small businesses or opened shops offered the young men their first job. 'People around here have happy memories of the Kobokan and are glad to help us,' said Mr Sato who obviously enjoyed putting people together to their mutual advantage. He went on, 'The four young men who live here have started a rock band. I am the lead singer,' he added modestly before bustling me into another change of slippers which even somewhere as dilapidated as the Kobokan's top floor required. The rock band, he explained, encouraged the young men to hang around the Kobokan rather than join the *bosozoku*, the motorcycle gangs which plagued the area and from which the *yakuza* picked new recruits.

Mr Sato was now walking very fast down a bare corridor throwing open doors then slamming them shut. I caught glimpses of small rooms empty of anything except sleeping bags and graffiti. One scrawl drew his attention. He pointed to it excitedly. 'Look!' he said, 'It's in English. These boys normally don't want to learn anything but they've got interested in the language because most rock lyrics are in English.' He contemplated the lines from 'Money for Nothing' happily then led me back on to the fire escape.

Mr Sato offered us lunch. Once a week the Kobokan provided a meal for thirty-five old people who now greeted us in the dining room. They were all very small, 5' or under, making me feel a giantess at 5' 8", and wore faded clothes, the women in a variety of mismatched prints. Most had gold teeth. Mrs Abe had told me, 'We Japanese care for the elderly. We respect them.' But these elderly lived alone on meagre pensions. The prospect of losing their independence terrified them. It meant banishment to a state nursing home which, because of the high price of land in central Tokyo, would be a two- or three-hour journey from family and friends. To keep themselves healthy, they exercised each morning, taking long walks or doing callisthenics in the local park. A group of them had worked out to the same exercise programme on the radio with the same friends in the same park since the 1930s. I thought they were sixty odd. In fact most were in their eighties and four in their nineties. I looked curiously at their worn, smiling faces. They had lived through an extraordinary period in Japan's history. They could recall the earthquake of 1923, had starved through the 1930s, survived the war, the bombings and the dislocation and then made possible Japan's formidable reconstruction in the decades that followed. They stared at me in equal fascination. It was hard to imagine a group of people with less in common.

Lunch proved a smart occasion with starched tablecloths, menus and a slide show. This last illustrated Mr Sato's trip to the States. He had gone to visit the original missionary group which had founded the Kobokan and to search out old documents relating to that period. First he showed a map of the Pacific to set the scene. There followed slides of the departure board at Narita airport with its list of exotic destinations. Mr Sato explained, 'We photographed every step of the way so that you can feel you are travelling with us.' The next slide revealed the interior of the plane

71

and the one after, an airborne Mr Sato now eating his lunch. 'Amazing isn't it,' said the old man next to me amid general explanations of wonder. My amusement gave way to admiration. Mr Sato had judged his audience nicely. None of these old people had ever been to an airport, let alone flown abroad.

We now moved on to photographs of America itself. Slides of American homes and gardens left the old people speechless. Finally my neighbour asked, 'Does just one family live in that mansion?' I nodded. 'An ordinary family?' he pursued. I said that it looked like an ordinary, middle-class home. The old man shook his head slowly. He was one of those who had failed to benefit from Japan's economic miracle. The old people fidgeted through photographs of the American missionaries. The last slide showed American missionaries staring with equal boredom at a map of Japan.

After lunch, to my surprise, we retired to a tatami room. I had not associated the cheerful chaos of the Kobokan with the elegance of tatami. The proceedings suddenly became formal. Mrs Nakamura, the social worker and myself knelt on one side of the table, Mr Sato and two workers on the other. Everyone slipped into traditional roles. Mr Sato sat straight backed and frowning. Mrs Nakamura executed a series of fluid movements on her knees to bring her opposite Mr Sato. Then with her hands placed at the correct angle on the mat, she bowed deeply. I began to have some inkling of what it took to be a lady in Japan.

They launched into discussion. From Mrs Nakamura's over-polite and increasingly vague Japanese, I guessed that an embarrassing situation had developed. The Kobokan had agreed to take me on but did I want them? Mrs Nakamura turned to me. 'Perhaps you would care to think about it and give an answer later,' she said. I had been in Japan long enough to understand that she required an immediate response. The whole room was waiting. Fortunately the Kobokan had interested me. 'Can I start next week?' I asked. I suggested that I might teach English to the rock band. Mr Sato sucked his teeth. The Kobokan, despite its eccentric air, did things in Japanese fashion. Newcomers began at the bottom. Working with the rock band obviously required a lengthy period of service. Mr Sato assigned me to the old people's lunch. I could help with the washing up. When I returned home and told Nida, she burst out laughing. 'I had better give you lessons,' she said.

After we left the Kobokan, the social worker offered to show me an alternative. Sumida-ku's official Community Centre proved to be an entirely new venture in a country which believes in providing only the basic welfare facilities. The contrast with the Kobokan which raised almost all its own funds, could not have been greater. The Community Centre soared up from the surrounding neighbourhood of small, old houses, a miracle in pink and chrome. Two suited officials showed us the facilities. Every room boasted an expensive appliance. Stroke victims relearnt basic skills in a bathroom whose floor rose and fell at the touch of a button or a kitchen where the stove, sink and even the work surfaces proved equally adjustable. The handicapped enjoyed a kiln, weaving looms (set on a platform laid with tatami) and a room devoted to carpentry all specially designed for their use. Automatic doors led to an airy dining room resplendent with plants.

The director told us proudly that the building was brand new but had taken ten years of discussion to reach fruition. 'But so beautiful now!' said Mrs Nakamura to cover the silence that followed this confession. Another question preoccupied me. The Kobokan, lacking as it did even the most elementary equipment, nonetheless had been full of people. We had walked around the entire building without encountering a soul. 'Where is everybody?' I blurted out. The director stared at me then began to blush. Mrs Nakamura erupted into gratitude as, with many bows, each getting progressively deeper, she hurried me from the place.

Once outside the social worker nodded at me in approval. In her view I had asked the right question. The officials, she explained, ran the community centre entirely for their own convenience. They needed time to write their reports before leaving at five o'clock. This meant closing the centre promptly at two. She went on, 'It cost so much, took so long to build and now it is only open half a day. The local people are very upset.'

On my return Nida remarked with her usual trenchancy, 'So you are paying me to clean your house while you clean up after old people in Sumida-ku?' To divert her attention I asked after a friend of hers who was marrying a Japanese. Nida did not view this as a cause for congratulation. 'She's mad' she said. I pointed out that it solved the problem of a work permit. Nida looked sideways at me. 'A Japanese!' she exclaimed. I asked what was wrong with them. Nida twisted the tip of the iron into the cuff of my husband's shirt. She hesitated then said shyly. 'We Filipinas are Christian. We enjoy sex with our husbands. Japanese give up having sex once they marry.' I asked how she knew. She explained that she had once worked part-time for a Japanese couple. The wife complained. 'She was a beautiful woman but the moment they married, he stopped having sex. He kept a mistress instead.' Many Japanese farmers, unable to attract Japanese wives, had married Filipinas. Nina said, 'When they divorce, the girl says that the life's too hard, the mother-in-law is not kind and so on, but it's none of those things; its the lack of sex.'

The doorbell rang for the third time that morning. Japanese housewives are importuned all day long by good-looking salesmen aware of the loneliness and, I now realized, the availability of their customers. Expecting the plumber, I ushered the Japanese man on the doorstep upstairs to my bathroom. He appeared nervous but so did most Japanese men confronted by me. At my bedroom, he baulked. 'This way, this way,' I said. He entered slowly and hesitated by the bed. I noticed he was blushing. 'In here,' I pointed to the bathroom. He stared at the tap. 'Broken,' I said in Japanese. Hesitantly he began to repair it. When he had finished, I offered to pay him. He grew agitated and insisted, like a child close to tears, that he speak to a Japanese. I said I could understand if he talked slowly. He shook his head. The situation appeared beyond him. He wanted one of his own to sort it out. Sympathizing with this, I took him next door to my neighbour.

Mrs Abe opened the door looking particularly fetching. Flowers

74

the same colour as her dress arched from a vase beyond her. To my surprise the plumber knew Mrs Abe and quickly launched into a story beyond my Japanese. Mrs Abe nodded and clicked her tongue several times. He was a young man whom distress made beautiful. 'What is it?' I interrupted impatiently. Mrs Abe turned to me, eyebrows raised. 'He said the offer of money is embarrassing. You see, he is not a plumber but a life insurance salesman. My life insurance salesman in fact. He is twenty minutes late,' she added and swept him into the house. Her policy took a great deal longer to sort out than my bathroom tap.

My entry into the Kobokan promised to introduce a side of Japanese life which I did not see in Shirogane. My daughter provided me with another opportunity. At the age of two she started at a Japanese nursery school. It proved as much an initiation ceremony for me as for her.

Mrs Abe's luncheon club expressed surprise at our choice. Their children attended private schools. *Hoikuen* are state run and means tested. They charged us according to how much income tax we paid. Started in 1920 for the offspring of factory workers and day labourers, they are open ten hours a day, some even on Sundays or at night for shift workers. They take children from four months to six years and, despite the high ratio of staff and excellent facilities, are considered by most Japanese a poor second to a mother's care. I went unwillingly. The *hoikuen* was my husband's idea. I had read about the Japanese education system and imagined an Orwellian set-up with babies peeing on demand.

'In which position does your child fall asleep?' asked two young teachers over Japanese tea. When I admitted I did not know, they expressed astonishment. 'All Japanese mothers sleep with their children,' they pointed out. I asked politely what the children learnt. Through the window I watched as three little girls cleaned out the cage of the school's pet rabbit. Did they engage in projects, I enquired. The young women looked puzzled. Projects, they asked, what were those? The children were taught when they asked to learn and not before. The teachers then handed me a report card for Gabriella. Each day they filled it in and sent it back for me to see. Each morning I had to write in Japanese what time Gabriella had gone to bed, how many hours she had slept, what she had eaten for breakfast and how she had played the night before. One item appeared to flummox the teachers. My friend who had come to help translate looked embarrassed. The teachers opened a dictionary, shook their heads then went in search of Miss Tanaka the headmistress, an attractive and intelligent woman in her early forties. Inspiration came suddenly to me. 'You mean pee pee and poo poo!' I exclaimed. 'Pee pee and poo poo,' Miss Tanaka repeated slowly. 'We did not learn that in my English conversation lessons,' sniffed my friend. 'Please note down the time of every dirty nappy,' said one young woman. 'And the contents,' added the other. So it was that I had to wake up early each morning in order to compose the Japanese characters for normal, runny or constipated.

The *hoikuen*, I now understood, initiated mothers into institutional life as surely as it did the child. I had imagined Japanese institutions forced new members into submission. I should have known, of course, that as with all things in Japan, submission is produced by seduction not coercion. The school itself delighted me. Clean, spacious and sunny with polished wooden floors, it opened on to a small park and even had a swimming pool. As I arrived each morning, children set off through the trees with bamboo cages to catch cicadas. Others helped Miss Tanaka erect a makeshift swing or lifted potatoes with the elderly gardener. Inside everyone, including the tea lady, bowed, smiled and greeted us by name. I found myself slipping into obedience as one would a hot bath. A deep bow of contrition is, after all, a novel form of penitence for messing up your child's threadworm test.

Gabriella, however, remained impervious, as the school birthday party proved. Held every month for children born during that period, Gabriella's occurred shortly after she started *hoikuen*. The whole school attended as well as parents of the birthday children. The teachers insisted I watched from a cupboard. Gabriella, they apologized, might see me and howl. First the older children came on to a stage made from two screens joined by a cardboard rainbow. The girls, both dressed as Minnie Mouse, sang songs and skipped while the boy, in a Robin Hood outfit, turned a somersault. Delighted parents inserted new film into their cameras and videos. I began to feel optimistic. I imagined Gabriella transformed into a Japanese child, docile and laughing. Then a teacher led her on stage. Everybody, from the smallest baby to the headmistress, wore a party hat except Gabriella who had thrown hers on the floor. The teacher tried to coax her into a bow. Instead she looked around the room of chanting children, seized her teacher's hand and pointed to the door. 'Out!' she announced. Her screams reverberated down the corridor. The other parents glanced at me pityingly. Certainly I made a pitiful sight, stuck in a cupboard with no camera and let down badly by a child who refused to join her group. Afterwards I found her singing 'London Bridge is Falling Down', surrounded by four exhausted Japanese teachers. On the last line they hesitated. 'Down,' repeated Gabriella until they collapsed obediently on to the floor.

Three months later Sport's Day saw even Gabriella integrated. It boasted an African theme. The small Japanese park had been transformed into an African jungle with cardboard animals and grass huts where the teachers sat. The trees were adorned with African masks and fetishes. Loudspeakers hanging in the branches blared African music. The headmistress, dressed in the purple robes of an African chief and waving a spear, led a band of children complete with raffia skirts, spears and war paint whooping around a cooking pot. To the side, kneeling on tatami mats spread out for the occasion, mothers gossiped and ate rice crackers. 'Everybody happy then!' proclaimed the loud speaker and we all applauded.

Only I stood out. A week beforehand a lifesize poster had appeared in the entrance hall instructing mothers how to dress. That morning I had dutifully wrapped myself in a sarong, hung African beads around my neck, put my hair up in a bandana and painted my face with Gabriella's felt-tip pens. The other mothers, unlike the park or the teachers, had resisted metamorphosis. Not one even sported a sarong let alone a face of orange, green and fluorescent pink. Even in Japan, it seems, there are limits to what a mother will do for her offspring. Mortified, I joined the parents seated on tatami mats. 'Shoes off,' said Gabriella sternly before I sat down and she added something in Japanese which made all the fathers laugh. It is very hard when your child tells a joke which you alone cannot understand. The parents ranged from very young fathers with punk hair styles to minute grandmothers in kimono. At least half were middle-class professionals. 'I wish the school was open on Saturday,' sighed one woman. 'I am so exhausted by then.' Another enquired about the British equivalent and was amazed when I admitted nothing similar existed. 'We spend money on juvenile delinquents instead,' I explained. 'What are those?' she asked. A tough little Japanese boy cupped Gabriella's face with his hands then chased her around a bush. She introduced him as her special friend. Sometimes, she added, they had their nappies changed together. His mother stared at me doubtfully then proffered a rice cracker.

Miss Tanaka, still resplendent in her African robes, sat down next to me. We watched Gabriella and her friend throw bean bags into the giant, brightly painted mouth of a crocodile. The school, I knew, stressed social abilities. From an early age the emphasis was on how to make friends and enjoy belonging to a group rather than fostering the individual skills encouraged in Western nursery schools. I asked Miss Tanaka what she considered most important. Her reply surprised me. She said, 'I want my children to learn how to enjoy life. That is very important. Afterwards. . .' she shrugged. I thought of what awaited them: the exam hell, the fabled ferocity of Japanese teachers, the bullying and the highest incidence of suicide amongst adolescents in the world. At the age of seven when they had to leave this arcadia how, I wondered, did the children adapt? Looking at my attire and painted face, all worn in a vain effort to blend in, Miss Tanaka said quietly, 'They can adapt later because they are happy here now.'

'Ah, you found your way!' exclaimed Mr Sato when I came to the Kobokan for the first time as a volunteer. Behind him four other volunteer workers, all women, lined up and bowed. They ushered me into the staff room, sat me down at a large table and proffered a cup of tea. It proved very sociable. The art master arrived with a box of stag beetles. A local electrician discussed the sumo tournament. As a child he had attended the After School Care Programme and now did all the Kobokan's electrical work for free. A young man offered to take me horse racing. Outside the nursery teachers pushed their charges, six to a cart, shouting and chanting past the window on the way to the park.

Mrs Goto, the lady in charge of lunch, handed me my first task. Each old person received a menu beautifully written and illustrated, the whole framed by a coloured border. My job was to cut out the menus, cut the coloured paper into larger squares and stick the first on top of the second, thirty-five times. Unfortunately I am unable to judge a straight line. Mrs Goto was a good-looking woman in her forties with a full figure and soft, thick hair. Her brother lectured on social work and this had aroused her interest. She had a lovely smile which she now tried on me. Again and again I adjusted the ruler. Finally, my hands damp with sweat, I drew the blade down. The edges frayed and tore. I then stuck the crooked menus on to the crooked pieces of paper and sat back. Mrs Goto peered over my shoulder. It had taken me a full hour to mess up her menus. Mrs Goto looked puzzled. Japanese children play with paper from an early age, folding it effortlessly into birds and animals. 'Perhaps you can do something else on your next visit?' she suggested hopefully. She used such a respectful form that it took several repetitions, both of us getting increasingly embarrassed, before I understood.

The following week Mrs Goto thought up a new strategy for coping with me. I was demoted from the menus to the *oshibori*, hot, damp flannels used to wipe the hands and face before a meal. I soaked the thirty-five *oshibori* in hot water, wrung them out, rolled them up into a sausage shape then laid each one in its own bamboo holder. This proved easy and a great relief after the menus.

When this was done I placed the *oshibori* on tablecloths washed and ironed every week by volunteer workers. 'Why not send them to the laundry?' I asked. Mrs Goto explained that the Kobokan could not afford laundries. They relied on volunteer workers, most of them women from the neighbourhood, to perform the smallest task. Mrs Goto showed me how to set the table attractively with the chopsticks, menus and *oshibori*. Another woman arranged flowers in a vase. These bright spots of colour and endeavour they hoped would overcome or at least camouflage the cracked walls and viewless windows, the lack of money and government indifference.

The old people arrived, slipping clumsily into the red slippers as we gave a shout of greeting. A small, tough woman in her sixties with two gold teeth introduced herself as Mrs Komita. Three times a week she came to the Kobokan at six o'clock in the morning to put out the rubbish. Did I know how to make Japanese tea, she asked, stabbing a rough and pudgy finger at the tea tray. I had heard nothing like her Japanese since my trip to Kabuki-cho. 'Hoity Toity!' she exclaimed at my verb endings and, shoving me aside as one might a docile cow, demonstrated how to make green tea. She placed three full cups on a tray and pushed me towards a group of old men who sat at a separate table from the women. 'Hurry up, hurry up,' she said, starting to fill the next row of cups. 'Do they always sit together?' I asked. 'Of course,' she replied surprised. 'What would we have to say to them?'

The arrival of tea endeared me to our visitors. The old men insisted I sit down and answer their questions. I asked if they had ever travelled abroad. One handsome old man remarked that he had been to Singapore 'during the war' then glanced at me guiltily. From his expression I guessed he might have been remembering his last encounter with a foreign woman. He fell silent. Then someone cracked a joke and he joined in the laughter with relief.

Suddenly Mrs Goto snatched up the *oshibori* and rushed to the staff room. I had failed to wring out the flannels sufficiently and a pool of water had formed at the centre of each tablecloth. I found Mrs Goto bent over the sink, the flannels piled up before her.

Overcome with embarrassment, I explained that it was my first attempt to prepare *oshibori*. 'We don't have them in England.' Mrs Goto stopped her frenetic wringing to stare at me. 'You have never done them before? You don't have them in England?' she repeated in amazement. 'They are only used in Japan,' I said. Mrs Goto called out to everyone in the room, 'Did you hear that! Only we Japanese use *oshibori*!' Then she turned back to me. 'What do you do instead in restaurants? How do you clean your hands?' I tried to think of an equivalent, loath to admit we lacked one. 'Well, everyone goes to the lavatory first and washes their hands there,' I said. Mrs Goto and I paused to imagine the scene. 'Fancy that,' she said politely.

I repeated the story to Mrs Abe who viewed my trips to the Kobokan as a manifestation of foreign eccentricity. She said, 'I always microwave mine.' I started to explain that the Kobokan possessed nothing like a microwave when I recalled the many times Mrs Abe had presented herself as the bastion of Japanese tradition. 'The old people are very fussy,' I lied. 'They know the difference between a microwaved *oshibori* and the hand-wrung version.' Mrs Abe fell silent. It was the first time I had discomforted her.

When I returned to the Kobokan the following week, Mr Sato explained they had not expected to see me again. They thought I had lost too much face. Japanese always underestimate the indifference of Westerners to making fools of themselves.

The wringing required to prepare the *oshibori* gave me blisters. Mrs Goto picked up my hand on one visit and exclaimed at the sores. She called over Mrs Komita. They compared my palms to their own, calloused from years of housework. 'She's never done anything in her life,' said Mrs Komita striking me lustily on the back. She and Mrs Goto burst out laughing and led me into the dining room to show my hands to the old ladies.

The Kobokan marked a new departure for me. Immersion into Japanese life, in spite of my blistered palms, became an attractive proposition.

4

J started at the Kobokan in the middle of summer. As Mrs Abe had emphasized, Japan enjoys four distinct seasons each celebrated enthusiastically by the Japanese with the appropriate food and festivals. These seasonal activities characterized life in Tokyo and provided much of its charm.

My favourite was summer. The sounds, sights and smells of a Japanese summer evoked the essence of the country and its past for me as no other time of the year. Summer released old Japan so pungently that anything modern or Western appeared to vaporize into the twilight. After a month's rainy season in June, an unbearable humidity fell upon the city. By August a short walk left one drenched in sweat. The city emptied and the air pulsated with the drilling of cicadas. Waste ground suddenly spurted dense entanglements of foliage. Black and white speckled mosquitoes bit even at midday and in the rain. Black butterflies as large as humming birds flitted through our garden. In the streets and parks boys in tight shorts carrying butterfly nets and plastic boxes pursued insects. The fireflies proved monstrous and well worth the pursuit. Young girls sported summer kimono in bright, flowered patterns and tied with a floppy red sash. Old men spent the hot evenings seated outside in their pyjamas or shuffling up the road in *yukata* and clogs. A sense of escape pervaded as if we had fallen into a time vacuum. The grown ups had gone away; the children were left to play.

That summer my husband was working very hard and I spent a

lot of time with Midori and Charlie. It provided an almost surreal contrast to my weekly visits to the Kobokan. Midori and I often had dinner together. I was instructing her on how to captivate Charlie: 'Play hard to get and concentrate on your career,' I repeated dinner after dinner. 'To be frank that is not quite how we do it in Japan,' she said as politely as she knew how. 'We want to make the man happy.'

I explained that my methods did have that effect, in the end. Midori shook her head. 'Charlie likes me to take care of him. He expects me to know what he wants without explanations.' I said briskly, 'That will get you nowhere.' Midori looked pained, 'Maybe not at first, but I have the example of my own parents.' She explained that her mother did everything for her father. For the first ten years of the marriage, he took it for granted. She never complained or demanded. Then gradually he came to rely on her. 'Now he does nothing without consulting her.' When they go out to lunch, he looks at her helplessly. '"You choose for me," he says.' I remarked, 'That's rather a long-term view. We have to get Charlie to propose first.' Midori bent forwards, a sheet of glittering hair shielding her face. I had been too forthright. 'Maybe that's impossible,' she said sadly.

After dinner we met Charlie and his friends at a party in a mock-Tudor house, one of the few Western-style houses in central Tokyo to survive the war and originally built by a wealthy politician. The party was to celebrate the birthday of Monday, a former girlfriend of Charlie's who was half Japanese and half Italian but looked Indian and liked to wear saris.

In a bare room with mullioned windows and parquet floor, a group of Japanese girls stood to one side dressed in the obligatory black. Too self-conscious to enjoy themselves they concentrated instead on doing the correct thing. At a bizarre party such as Monday's, this proved confusing. They watched stony-faced as I discussed vending machines which sold schoolgirl uniforms to the perverted with a man from Manchester dressed in a red plastic suit. They muttered when I danced with a Japanese film star who introduced himself by shooting me with a cap gun. Finally a broker friend of Charlie's offered one of them a drink. This animated all the girls. They immediately broke into the routine of giggling, hands over the mouth and tossing of hair. Charlie said to me, 'They're like dolls. You just pick them up and put them down. If Midori left me, I could ring about half a dozen girls at any time of the night and they would get out of bed, come round and get into mine.'

Soon afterwards we left the party for a club featuring a transvestite evening. The transvestites were students at Keiyo university and the sons of some of Tokyo's oldest and richest families. They were putting on the show for kicks. A queue waited outside. The man from Manchester disappeared to find the manager. Two young men dressed as temple dancers from Thailand barred our way. They wore elaborate, pointed crowns and their arms, necks and legs were encased in gold jewellery. 'It's full,' said one slowly batting three-inch metallic eyelashes at me. On his chest rotated a disc displaying the signs of the zodiac and flashing lights. Below this he wore a gold G-string set off by pink suspenders and pink, fishnet stockings. The manager of the club appeared. Entranced by the sight of Monday descending the staircase, her arms full of lilies, he let us in.

We groped down a black passage to a door which opened to reveal a high-ceilinged, crowded room. A video projected hard porn movies on to a brick wall. Transvestites danced on platforms at head level. One wore nothing but silver hoops squeezed one on top of the other up to the chest where sprouted tiny, hormone-induced breasts. Others flaunted nipples beneath magnifying glass balls. 'These can't all be students,' I protested to Midori as we pushed through the crowds. 'Oh no, they are professionals from Osaka,' she shouted. 'So cute aren't they?' Charlie was passing around a magnum of champagne as he danced with five or six brokers in the middle of the floor. Midori tried to join in but he spun away, catching the eye of a transvestite swaying above in black leather, before starting a slam dance with one of his male friends.

Against a wall I met a Lebanese girl who told me it was difficult to have sex in Tokyo. Over her head the video showed a blond man sticking his erect penis through a hole in the wall of a public lavatory. Suddenly a change in the lighting announced the start of a review. We all stopped dancing and sat around the floor like children waiting for a story. A transvestite made up to resemble Julie Andrews and wearing a high-necked, purple dress tripped under the lights. As a view of alpine flowers replaced that of a man sucking himself off, the transvestite burst into 'The hills are alive with the sound of music'. Pierre had just arrived with Annunciation. He turned to me in bafflement. 'What is "The Sound of Music" please?' he asked.

The Japanese attitude towards sex, a pleasure like eating or drinking, ensured that Tokyo nightlife, even at its most lurid, rarely lapsed into sleaze. Sleaziness is an offshoot of the Western sense of shame and the Japanese have no shame where sex is concerned. It meant even the most outrageous spots exuded an air of genuine glee. Tokyo nightlife evoked those first forays into the adult world when menace and disillusion are still a distant proposition. This proved to be a quality of Japan in general. Here was a consequence of living in a hierarchical society: Japan rendered us perpetual adolescents. We lost our independence but escaped accountability. In exchange for accepting authority, authority took care of us. As long as I tried my best and apologised when I failed, I received a degree of indulgence unknown in the West. I was enjoying a cartoon-strip existence of excitement and adventure where a whack on the head caused no more harm than an explosion of stars. I began to dread the return to London and resumption of adulthood.

I felt this strongly at the Kobokan. The old people had never encountered a foreigner before. They adopted me as a mascot. The depth of emotion took me by surprise. The process stripped off an outer layer of skin and left me childlike and trusting. I sought to empathize with every nuance of their behaviour without really understanding what this entailed. It was the Takahashis, however, who provided a clue.

I had been discussing the latest banking scandals with one old lady who attended the Kobokan lunches. Mrs Takahashi had large eyes and a competent air. In her day, she remarked, banks had been much less free and easy with their funds. In 1947 her husband needed to borrow money to start a small business making weighing machines. They had no collateral, 'but my husband's an honest and sincere man so I said, "Go and at least see the bank manager. He might take to you."' Mr Takahashi sat opposite the bank manager and explained with increasing embarrassment what he hoped to achieve compared to the little he possessed. The bank manager stared hard at him. 'Show me your hands,' he commanded. Mr Takahashi held them out. They were calloused and cracked. 'Those are the hands of a hard-working man,' said the manager. 'I will lend you the sum you want.' Intrigued, I asked if I could meet Mr Takahashi. Here was a representative of the thousands of ordinary Japanese who had forged Japan's economic miracle.

'That might be difficult,' said Mr Sato who appeared surprised and embarrassed by my request. Finally he said I could go but only if accompanied by himself and Mrs Goto. It was my turn for embarrassment. Mrs Goto had to travel an hour to get to the Kobokan and Mr Sato, I knew, could barely spare the time. 'Can't I go on my own?' I asked but this appeared unthinkable. What I had imagined as a relaxed chat had turned into a formal delegation.

Mrs Takahashi met us at the door and led us nervously upstairs to a spacious, light room. Mr Takahashi stood up and bowed to us. I suddenly understood everyone's trepidation over this meeting. Mr Takahashi was a small but formidable man with large hands and ears that stuck out. We sat down on the floor. Mr Takahashi sat straight-backed and unyielding, the famous hands placed firmly on the table between us. Behind him a stuffed pheasant with a tentative expression perched on a rock in a glass case. On the balcony sunflowers, marigolds and hydrangeas formed a dense screen between the Takahashis and the outside world.

Mr Takahashi had grown up in a village in Chiba. In 1930 at

the age of fifteen an uncle found him a job in a Tokyo shop which also provided food and accommodation. He slept with ten other boys in a bunkroom waking up at six in the morning and working until six in the evening. Once a month he got the first and third Sunday off. I nodded sympathetically. Mr Takahashi looked at me surprised. Compared to life in a Japanese village, working twelve hours a day in a shop 'was like a festival every day of the year. Why, we even got meat about twice a week! I had never eaten meat in my village or dreamt I ever would!' After work he and the other assistants studied for about two hours. On his day off he slept. 'It was my favourite pastime. I was always tired. I didn't have the energy to do sports. When I see how my grandson fritters away his time. . .' His wife caught his eye. Mr Takahashi paused then went on, 'Of course I can't comment as it just becomes a source of argument. But the difference between his experience and mine! How can he imagine, spoilt and rich as he is, what it was like. Why,' he spluttered, 'he's never even been cold!' Mrs Takahashi and I made soothing noises. Mr Takahashi relaxed, glanced at me approvingly and even let his large reptilian mouth break into a glimmer of a smile.

He was paid 18 yen a month, he continued. The shop kept back 13.5 yen for board and lodging. Of the 4.5 yen left, the shop automatically deducted 2 yen towards his savings. That left 2.5 yen for Mr Takahashi. 'Everyone assumed it was a good idea that we were made to save. I think they should have allowed us to spend it on food. We were always hungry.' After the war and a spell in China, he returned to his village and started a business transporting rice to Tokyo. At this point in his story a Takahashi daughter-in-law arrived with lunch, black lacquered boxes of sushi or raw fish, an expensive delicacy which amazed Mrs Goto and Mr Sato. I started eating enthusiastically, praising the fish which endeared me further to Mr Takahashi. When his wife left us to fetch more tea, I thought I had made sufficient progress to pose a personal question. 'Please ask how he met his wife,' I said to Mr Sato who was translating. Mr Sato winced. 'We Japanese don't ask personal questions,' whispered Mrs Goto to me.

To Mr Sato's obvious relief, Mr Takahashi replied readily. His wife had come from the next-door village. His brother worked with her father and had arranged a meeting at her parents' house. At that time, explained Mr Takahashi, such a visit was tantamount to a proposal of marriage as a rejection would cause his brother to lose too much face. 'So you had to trust the person making the introduction!' There were six people in the room and the young couple barely exchanged a word, 'but my first impression was "Not bad" and in those days first impressions provided the answer! I didn't care about anything else. I just liked the look of her!' Here, much to everyone's amazement, Mr Takahashi broke into a huge smile.

Mrs Takahashi returned to the room and I asked her the same question. She collapsed into giggles, 'Frankly, I wanted someone a bit taller,' she said. 'His brother was so tall and good looking. I rather liked him.' Undeterred by this, Mr Takahashi lifted up the tablecloth. It was, he explained, the same table over which fifty years ago they had first met. Mr Sato, astounded by this unexpected side of Mr Takahashi, began to laugh. 'So romantic!' exclaimed Mrs Goto. At the end of the interview Mr Takahashi drove us back to the Kobokan. 'He bought a new car for his wife because he was worried about her health,' explained Mrs Goto. 'Very sweet, don't you think?'

The next week, Mr Sato took me aside. Mrs Takahashi had rang up to say that, in all their years of marriage, she had never seen her husband so animated. Never before had he condescended to eat with guests or offer them a lift home. He usually kept himself to himself, 'it's just his character,' she remarked. He had enjoyed the visit immensely. 'No one's shown an interest in his past before,' she went on. Later I discovered that Mr Sato had once rescued the Takahashi grandson when he got into bad company. The reclusive Mr Takahashi had only agreed to see me because he owed Mr Sato a big favour. Now I understood the reason for Mr Sato's unease. Unwittingly I had blundered into one of the many webs of obligation that stretch between the Japanese.

My simple request had left me beholden to so many people, I was unsure where even to begin.

Not all my meals proved as complicated or as Japanese in character. Beneath swathes of plastic vines in a German bierkeller off Ropongi, platters of curry were giving off an intoxicating smell. In the kitchen three Ethiopian women, their hair coiled on top of their heads like tiaras, prepared more food. They were wives of diplomats from the Ethiopian embassy and part of a novel scheme for making money. The expense of life in Tokyo had forced many Third World embassies to close down. The Ethiopian embassy hoped to avoid this fate by opening a restaurant. To test the market they were holding an Ethiopian lunch to which a Malawian friend had invited me. The wives admitted they cooked for free, explaining the optimism of the restaurant's owner.

I carried my food upstairs and squeezed into a wooden banquette opposite a red-faced Englishman with a massive head of white hair and white sideburns. He was growling about 'the good old days' in Japan with the nostalgia of a foreigner who had first arrived in the 1950s when Westerners were a novelty and treated with respect. His general irritation with the world indicated that this was no longer the case.

He introduced himself as Mr Pickles. His companion, an elegant Japanese in his sixties, was a member of the Diet, spoke French and German and, he made clear to me, had a penchant for blondes. When he left to fetch me a glass of wine, Mr Pickles leaned forward. 'He's too international to get on in Japanese politics,' he confided, shaking his jowls. He explained that the MP's career had ended while in charge of the government department seeking to discover the cause of landslides. The officials had made a small hill, started a landslide and killed nine technicians. When told of the disaster the MP exclaimed, 'Mon Dieu!' He was sacked not so much for his department's incompetence – 'No one minded that!' – but for his reaction, so French and alien.

The MP returned and resumed chatting me up. This took the

form of admonishment. He explained that homosexuality did not exist in Japan because 'our women are so accommodating'. He gave me a meaningful look. Accommodation was a virtue he hoped I possessed. Western women's aggression, he added, was the cause of homosexuality in the West. Mr Pickles, in whom drink had unloosened a spirit of mischief, exclaimed, 'That's rubbish and I want you to meet someone who can prove it.' He then reached out and grasped the arm of a thin, wispy haired Englishman seeking to pass us.

The man, introduced as Tom, was sufficiently drunk to be utterly honest. 'I am a homosexual,' he said earnestly to the MP, 'and I can assure you that Tokyo boasts more homosexuals than any city that I have ever lived in.' To prove his point he recounted his adventures in Tokyo's bath houses, bars and back streets. 'Tokyo is a sexual Disneyland. Its all so clean and available,' he added. The MP at once became tight and cross and attempted to escape by flirting with me. This only elicited more scandalous stories from Tom and lectures from Mr Pickles on the Japanese lack of morality. The MP grew very angry indeed. 'We Japanese are the most honourable race in the world,' he burst out. 'What about World War II,' snarled Mr Pickles. The MP rose from the table and with barely a nod at me, departed.

Mr Pickles went on to savage Japanese bureaucrats and politicians adding, 'The only immorality in this city lies in being found out.' He was one of a number of foreigners who had lived a long time in Japan. He spent years learning the language only to discover that he had made his career in a country which he now hated. Initial enthusiasm had given way to disillusionment with the oppressive nature of Japanese society. 'I loved Japan until I knew enough Japanese to read the newspapers,' is how one famous American translator put it. I often wondered what the Japanese made of this behaviour: one moment fawned over, the next despised. 'They did for my best friend, the Prince, you know,' said Mr Pickles darkly before he too departed, bulldozing his way out, a glass of wine still in hand.

I found myself alone in the banquette with an unlikely couple.

A small Ethiopian who wore a red jersey and matching carnation introduced as his friend a middle-aged Japanese lady dressed in kimono. She had a broad, serene face and announced herself as a housewife who did calligraphy 'as a hobby'. At this the Ethiopian shook his head. 'She is a magnificent artist,' he said and pulled from his wallet a photograph of her work. A single character meaning 'Joy' erupted then seemed to shimmer and finally diffuse like a view in the heat of summer. I asked to see more. Mrs Yamada suggested we could visit a nearby restaurant which had bought one of her works.

The restaurant was Japanese and very expensive. Mrs Yamada refused to come in with us. She explained, 'My agent told me to keep a low profile. Japanese dismiss work executed by a woman. They are not going to buy art from a housewife!' The Ethiopian and I stood side by side and stared at the 7' high character in black ink. It was powerful and almost abstract in its intensity. I tried and failed to imagine it exploding from a brush held by Mrs Yamada. 'What must she really be like!' I finally exclaimed. The Ethiopian sighed. He was obviously smitten by the calligrapher.

Outside I arranged to see Mrs Yamada again. She was coming to Shirogane the following week to play bingo for the first time with some Americans. We agreed to meet for tea. On the day Mrs Yamada telephoned to cancel. She had won first prize and could not leave until the presentation at the end. She felt sure I would understand. It was a bread mixer and just what she had always wanted.

It had become so hot that I tended to stay indoors during the day. In late afternoon when the heat had abated, I walked down a narrow road shaded by trees to a swimming pool. On one side stood a wooden temple encircled by hundreds of stone idols the size of large dolls. Their faces, weathered and overgrown with moss, stared out from beneath pink cotton bonnets and matching bibs. Some held plastic windmills which rustled in the breeze. On the other side I glimpsed through a hedge a hotel garden set with tables and chairs beneath parasols. Sometimes a band practised jazz.

Other afternoons against the din of cicadas and the cawing of Tokyo's crows I caught the eerie twinkling of bells from the temple designed to entrap the breeze and give the listener an illusion of coolness.

Mrs Abe explained that the idols symbolized stillbirths. There seemed an awful lot for a country with the lowest infant mortality rate in the world. Later I learnt the true story. After women have abortions, they raise an idol to their dead foetus. The Japanese government allows two forms of contraception: the condom and abortion. The government has assured Japanese women that they are physically different from Western women and therefore unsuited to the contraceptive pill. The truth behind this lie is that those Japanese doctors whose high incomes arise from performing abortions have persuaded the government to keep the pill out of Japan. And so the sad little figures continue to proliferate.

In the middle of August, the Japanese celebrate Obon, the festival of the dead. Tokyo is left empty as Japanese return to their home towns and villages to sweep the graves of their ancestors. It is a time of festivals and firework displays. Young men naked but for loin cloths carry the local shrine through the streets. At night slow, hypnotic folk dances take place to the beat of a drum struck by the local strongmen.

This is the season for ghost stories. The attendant shivers are meant to cool the listener. Mrs Abe provided me with one when I dropped by to discuss the plum bonsai whose leaves had been munched by a caterpillar. Mrs Abe reassured me and introduced her friend, a self-effacing woman in her sixties. She left soon after, Mrs Abe wishing her a good trip. 'Where is she going?' I asked idly. 'To her fiancé's house,' replied Mrs Abe. I remarked that she seemed a bit old to be having a fiancé. 'He died in the war,' said Mrs Abe, then explaining that the couple had not enjoyed an official engagement merely an understanding. After the war she had married a man who had neglected her and often been violent. He had died about fifteen years before. Shortly after the funeral she had encounted the mother of her former sweetheart. It was August and stifling in Tokyo. The woman invited her to stay in their country house. Drawn to the old couple whose son she associated with the happiest period of her life, she accepted the invitation. When she arrived they put her to sleep in their son's room. Mrs Abe hesitated, unable to express herself. Finally she said, 'I bumped into her a week later in Tokyo. She was a woman transformed. She radiated happiness. I had never seen her like that before.' Her friend explained that during the night the ghost of her former fiancé had visited her. They talked for hours. 'Every year since then she spends Obon with the old couple and sleeps in her fiancé's room; and every year he comes to her.' Mrs Abe fell silent. Recounting the story to a foreigner had made her see it in a new light. She admitted, 'You know, until your interest I never thought of it as strange. You saw for yourself. She's such an ordinary woman!'

The British provided a more prosaic view of a Japanese summer. At the Yokohama Country Club, in the former treaty port and forty-five minutes' drive through Tokyo's industrial sprawl, a cricket pitch sat on the bluff overlooking the harbour. Beneath a blue canopy wives and girlfriends watched the match and gossiped during the long periods of inactivity. If it had not been so humid, some of us might have knitted. The players wore an array of creams and whites while the umpire sported bare legs and sandals. Fielders chewed grass or picked old mosquito bites unless they felt the eyes of their women upon them. Then they straightened up or crouched down and stared alertly at the batsman.

At lunchtime a very old Japanese in a straw hat carried a broom on to the pitch and dusted the stumps. Two equally old English-men in shorts with thick, red necks followed behind. One patted his stomach as he passed me. 'It all came on in three months and I have never got it off,' he confided as they inspected the pitch together. Beneath the canopy a Japanese waiter in a bow tie collected empty glasses.

Just before tea, an American broker led a curious group of Japanese and South Americans over. They looked at us, then at the pitch, then back at us again. Finally they turned to the American for an explanation. He said, 'This is the English playing cricket.' Wives and girlfriends straightened their backs and turned their attention to the pitch. We all stared fixedly. Nothing happened.

Over the Obon weekend Midori invited Charlie and my family to stay at her family house on the coast. The Japanese seaside around Tokyo is something to avoid. The once beautiful rocky outcrops and small, steeply sided bays now lie beneath motorways, *pachinko* parlours and hotels. As with most trips into Japan's so-called wilderness, we prepared ourselves for disappointment.

Midori told us to drive along the sea road lined on both sides with buildings until we reached a green field. 'A green field,' said my husband, 'you must have misheard.' But into a green field we nonetheless turned and parked. Lying below the road, hidden by a hedge and shaded by pine trees, stood a Japanese house looking out over the sea. In silence we picked our way across the slabs of stone to the porch. It was a place of enchantment.

The house proved old and rickety. A wooden balcony and shoji screens enclosed three tatami rooms, a bathroom and a kitchen. We pushed back the screens to reveal the garden and a view over trees to the shoreline where a twisted pine grew from a rock surrounded by sea. When I enthused over the house's simplicity, imagining it had been in the family for generations, Midori said, 'My grandfather bought it in a housing show. It was designed by a famous architect in the Kyoto style.'

We walked down through the trees to the beach. The tide was out revealing rocky outcrops. We waded out to one, clambered up and sunbathed, silenced, after weeks in Tokyo, by this sudden expanse of sky and sea.

Afterwards we took a bath in the *ofuro*, a stone tub now equipped with plumbing. 'Until a few years ago we heated the water the old-fashioned way by lighting a fire underneath,' explained Midori. She cooked dinner in the small, primitive kitchen off the house. The floor and sink were of stone. Midori kept everything scrupulously clean. Charlie watched in silence as she chopped vegetables and gutted fish. She had the ability to make the food look aesthetically pleasing at every stage of its preparation. She glanced up at Charlie and pointed to the courtyard beyond the kitchen. 'Please cook the fish just how I say,' she instructed. Charlie went out smiling. He had never seen her in a Japanese setting before. She had always been an appendage to his world. She displayed an authority and tranquility he had not known she possessed.

We got very drunk over dinner and I went to bed early. A few hours later I had to brave the Japanese lavatory. This consists of a hole in the ground over which you crouch. It requires strong thighs and is uncomfortable and cold even when designed in wood by Midori's grandfather. Afterwards I returned to our room, my feet silent on the tatami. Midori had left the shoji screen open to reveal a new moon tilted like a jewel above the rock and the fir tree. Charlie leaned against the shoji frame staring up at the sky. From the hunch of bedclothes on the floor, Midori stole towards him on her knees. Close to, she hesitated. He turned and smiled, then seeing her look of enquiry he held out his arms and drew her to him. I crept back to my futon.

5

As autumn approached, the weather grew cooler. At this time of the year Japanese plan their annual hike into the countryside. The Kobokan proved no exception. Mrs Goto invited my family for a day out in Kamakura, a temple town an hour by train from Tokyo. Mrs Goto explained that the art master knew the area well and would be able to find a walk for us far from the crowds. I packed a picnic and instructed my husband to say nothing about either my journalism or our Filipina maid. He asked why. I said, 'I don't want my friends to think I am different.' He looked at me oddly. I was expressing a very Japanese sentiment.

We met outside Kamakura station. My hopes to blend in were immediately shattered. The Japanese wore identical hiking outfits of plus fours, patterned socks, mountain boots and a cloth cap. They looked curiously at my husband, a foot taller than anyone else, unshaven and in shorts. With relief they turned to my daughter. 'Isn't she cute!' they exclaimed. Gabriella burst into tears.

The countryside proved hardly isolated. Most of Tokyo had decided to take a walk around Kamakura that Sunday. We queued to scramble up the narrow paths and joined crowds admiring the view from rocky outcrops. The art master picked one of these for our lunch. Mrs Goto and the other ladies laid out plastic sheets and bamboo mats. We sat down and helped ourselves to *bento* (lunch) boxes filled with egg, rice and grilled fish. Everyone had made a speciality except for me. I had brought sandwiches, the bread cut too thick, the fillings half lost at the bottom of the bag. The Japanese helped themselves cautiously. 'Brown bread!' they exclaimed in surprise. None of them had eaten brown bread before. Gabriella shook her head. She preferred Mrs Goto's rice and seaweed balls. 'So good,' chorused the Japanese approvingly. The art teacher unpacked a spirit lamp and made coffee. We drunk it surrounded by slowly moving crowds of people unsure whether to stare at the view or the curious sight we offered.

When we got up to leave, Mrs Goto looked at me then at herself and burst out laughing. My husband bore both Gabriella and our knapsack. I held nothing. Mrs Goto, on the other hand, carried numerous parcels and plastic bags. Her husband walked freely, swinging his arms and whistling. 'Japanese tradition,' I said pointing to him. He beamed at my overladen husband. 'British tradition,' he announced with satisfaction. Mrs Goto repeated this to everyone for months afterwards. It more than made up for my family's eccentric food and clothes.

'This is the first time I have felt this love feeling,' Midori admitted to me. We were sitting in Midori's favourite sushi bar, a small, cramped place that could fit no more than ten people at a time. It stayed open until four in the morning. We were discussing the strange turn which Midori's affair with Charlie had taken. Midori had no one else in whom to confide. At a loss both culturally and emotionally she had appointed me as her guide through the alien territory in which she now found herself.

An English or American girlfriend might have revealed sexual details. Midori merely remarked that at the point when it had become, 'less interesting', Charlie had fallen in love with her. 'I was expecting the affair to end. I was even looking for somewhere else to live and now this!' She never ran her hands through her hair like a Western woman. Instead she turned up the ends of one glistening cluster and inspected it as a housewife might a favourite ornament. Satisfied with what she saw, she looked up. 'He's very young,' I cautioned. Midori pointed out that most Japanese men were married by twenty-seven. Embarrassed by her expectations, I asked what made Charlie so different from previous Japanese lovers or even her husband.

She wrinkled up her forehead. Intensely practical, she found herself unable to describe love in abstract terms. Finally she said, 'He comes home before eight and we eat dinner together. We talk, many funny things. He has a funny way of expressing himself, don't you think? He calls me his Little Demon, makes me put on my demon face and hiss like a kettle. Then after dinner we go to bed.' She saw my expression, 'Not for sex things, Harriet. We don't do any of that.' 'Well what do you do?' I asked. 'We watch samurai drama on the television. We play a game. Who is next to be killed. He reads *The Financial Times*. I can't sleep with the light on so I wait until he finishes. Then we go to sleep together, always hugging tight.' She shook her head in wonder, 'So sweet don't you think?'

I said, 'Its called companionship. Don't you have that in Japan?' Across the counter, the sushi bar owner waited as we decided what to order next from the slices of raw fish, the crab legs and minute bamboo boxes of fish egg and sea urchin which lay before us. 'You're eating so much, you'll burst,' he said crossly. He preferred the drinkers that squeezed us from either side. I found the physical proximity of strangers in a sushi bar intensely soothing. They made no demands. The man whose body pressed into mine would never address a word to me or even catch my eye. Midori continued, 'Charlie tells me all the time how beautiful I am. He says I should be as proud as a queen. He also says I should read more, but to be truthful it is so tiring in English.'

The wife of the sushi bar owner handed us each a soup made of cockle shells to finish the meal. She stood until the early hours by the soup pot behind her husband. I leaned forward and asked why she did not chop fish. Her husband roared with laughter. 'Man's work,' he answered for her as he pared a slither of mackerel. He wiped his strong, fat fingers then flipped the mackerel on to a portion of rice and sprinkled the whole with shreds of ginger. He explained, 'It takes years to learn how to cut fish.' From behind his back his wife smiled faintly then resumed her stare into nothing.

Mrs Abe was widowed and rarely talked about her husband. Apart from his family background I understood he had been a disappointment. His career had failed to progress and they had had twin daughters, doubly unlucky in a country that favours sons. Mrs Abe shared her house, uneasily I gathered, with her widowed father-in-law. One morning I saw him in our local vegetable shop. The shop owner was picking out punnets of mushrooms for old Mr Abe while the two men discussed the latest financial scandal. Mr Abe carried a hooded falcon on his wrist. At his feet sniffed a beagle. Nobody, apart from me, showed surprise at this sight. I introduced myself and asked about the bird. After this I often met Mr Abe on the way to the hospital grounds behind our house. In its relative wilderness he flew the falcon and let the dog snuffle through the bushes after cats.

Mr Abe had white hair and possessed a high-pitched voice which resembled the mew of his falcon. He belonged to one of Japan's oldest and most powerful families. He was a mild man who nonetheless knew all the gossip. He dismissed Mrs Kobayashi's husband, the top banker, as 'a rather noisy man'. He preferred birds and animals to people. Shortly after I had presented him with some wildlife videos, Mrs Abe came over wearing a puzzled expression. Her father-in-law wished to invite us to his family's country villa to view the maples. Her tone implied this had not been her idea.

As Mrs Abe drove us down, she impressed my husband with the grandeur of her late husband's family. In the back old Mr Abe and I discussed Japanese monkeys. He had once visited a hot spring in the north of Japan during winter. There he had found a family of monkeys ensconced in the steaming water. Snow covered the ground. 'Each monkey wore a hat of snow flakes,' squeaked Mr Abe cupping his hands over his head. His daughter-in-law glanced at us in the car mirror then resumed her lecture.

The villa stood on the outskirts of a castle town surrounded by the countryside of Mrs Abe's dreams. We drove past Japanese farmhouses the size of barns with roofs of towering thatch. Paddy fields reflected the small, forested mountains that rose above them. Various species of tree grew from the mountainsides at different angles, creating a textured patchwork effect. Plumes of giant bamboo swayed between oak and dark troughs of pine. Hawks, as common as sparrows, hovered overhead. Further north the leaves had begun to turn, the red and gold tinging the green of the colder valleys with a sudden impression of fire.

We drove to the old part of town where a wide, shallow river separated the merchant from the samurai quarter. Four hundred years ago the Tokugawa shogunate fixed everyone's place in society. While the samurai assumed a position of privilege even the peasant ranked above the merchant. In practice the samurai borrowed money from the merchant and married into his family when the debts became insuperable. Rank dictated the size and position of a man's house. The homes of the merchants occupied a series of narrow streets. Forbidden the grand entrance and high walls of the samurai's residence, they were built of black wood against which a pot of wall flowers, a small fir tree and a trough of lilies shone with eerie brilliance.

We crossed the river. Carp swam in the clear water. On the river bank market stalls displayed rows of minute aubergines, kimonos for babies and vats of spices, as well as coiled snakes and dried monkey heads for the sick. On the edge of the samurai quarter looking out over the mountains stood the Abe residence surrounded by a stone wall topped with three rows of glazed tiles. We drove through the gate. A Japanese villa and garden lay before us.

Mrs Abe suggested that we walk around the garden first. It contained a lake fed by two artificial streams. In spring the irises planted along the banks flooded the channels with blue. In autumn the overhanging branches of the Japanese maples created a burning red tunnel. About the garden pine trees and wisteria had been pruned into fantastic shapes. Some had boughs propped up by wooden crutches or held aloft with a tent of ropes. Upon the branch of one tree a very old man in a straw hat and the jodhpurs

101

and split-toed leggings of the Japanese workman trimmed back new growth with a pair of scissors. Mrs Abe explained, 'Five gardeners work here full time. Every tree requires painstaking pruning.' She then snapped out an order. The old man clambered down his ladder and with much bowing hurried us to where a white canopy in a corner of the garden sheltered pots of chrysanthemums, the old man's speciality. Each plant had been grown over a steel frame, the size and shape of a crinoline. The buds poking through this construction would produce 112 blooms, he told us proudly, to create a pyramid of flowers and a magnificent sight. 'We Japanese enjoy a unique love of nature,' said Mrs Abe. The construction before us revealed the opposite. In Japan a flower or tree is only beautiful when twisted into something else. The countryside is scarred with the attempt, the gardens paeons to artifice. It is the imposition of man's will on nature rather than nature itself which delights the Japanese.

We stopped to admire a waterfall, its stones arranged to produce a splashing soothing to the ear and a hill covered with moss which had taken 100 years to reach its present peak of velvety perfection. 'Japanese gardens do not have as many flowers as yours,' said Mrs Abe as if in need of an excuse. I glanced at her. She wore the faint smile of a woman who has just dealt a back-handed compliment. Flowers, unless trained chrysanthemums, would have been too easy.

Mr Abe was contemplating a pair of swans on the lake. They would not take to each other, he explained shaking his head in mystification. So acrimonious had become their disputes that Mr Abe had separated them with a sluice gate. This appeared to have worked. Each swan swam around its watery allotment ignoring the other. Mrs Abe dabbed her lips impatiently with a handkerchief then led us to the house.

She opened a door from the garden. 'Western style,' she said and stood back complacently. My husband and I did not know what to say. The room, like the garden, was the work of her husband's grandfather. Ninety years before, the industrial magnate had gone on a shopping spree to Europe and brought back a grandfather clock, heavy furniture, stuffed animal heads and alabaster nudes. Everything was ugly. 'What a contrast to outside,' I finally managed to say. Mrs Abe pushed in a trolley laid with an Edwardian silver service. She gave us coffee and sandwiches made of white bread that tasted of cotton wool. 'I don't want to put the servants to any trouble,' she said.

While we ate, I asked Mr Abe about his parents. He cocked his head on one side, resting his chin on his finger tips. 'Old-fashioned,' he said of his mother. 'She never expressed an opinion. In front of my father she behaved as meekly as a housemaid repeating, "Yes, yes" to everything.' His father had exercised complete power. He rarely went to the office, preferring to spend long periods in his study. The household revolved around his whims. Mr Abe explained that it was the norm in most Japanese families until the 1950s when men began to work eighteen hours a day at the office. In their absence they lost domestic authority. Mr Abe reached for a sandwich and held it between two fingers next to his ear. He went on. 'Wife and children consider father a nuisance. They don't want him there. No one pays attention to his opinions or needs.' Mr Abe bit mournfully into his sandwich then observed, 'In the newspapers they say some wives wash their husband's underwear separately from the rest of the family. Can you imagine such a thing? They complain men are dirty.' Mrs Abe breathed in sharply. I dared not look at her face. Mr Abe had put the sandwich back on his plate after the one bite. 'Egg has a queer taste for me,' he apologized looking past his daughter-in-law. 'I have found that so for some years now.'

I observed how pleasant it must have been to have his father so much at home. What had they done together? Mr Abe thought for a long time. Finally he recalled one expedition father and son made every New Year's Day to a favourite geisha house. On that day the women dressed in black kimono and wore hair pins decorated with rice leaves. For special patrons like Mr Abe's father they performed a dance which Mr Abe described as 'ravishing'. Afterwards his father gave him twenty envelopes containing a New Year's gift of money which the boy handed to each of the women. Mr Abe folded his hands in his lap with a curiously feminine gesture of defeat and sighed, 'Those days are all over. Wives don't let husbands spend money on geisha now.' A silence ensued which Mrs Abe broke by suggesting we leave. She had no intention of showing us the rest of the house. The Western room was as far as we were allowed to penetrate.

On the way out Mrs Abe confided in a voice loud enough to be overheard by both men that her friend, Mrs Tashiro, had also visited geisha houses with her father as a young girl. 'After her marriage of course she had to give that up. The first time her husband went with colleagues from his company, the women all exclaimed, "You are Miss Yamaguchi's new husband! Please give her our best regards." He was not pleased.' She gave a big smile. It was obviously one of her favourite stories. Ahead of us Mr Abe had stopped to feed the cob. Even the prospect of food could not entice the hen to his side. 'Silly bird,' said Mrs Abe.

As we walked around the neighbourhood, I noticed a stream running next to the Abe property. Mr Abe stared at the rushing water pensively. He explained that he had often played here as a child to escape the servants. He went on, 'Servants enjoyed a lot of power in an old family like mine. They never got sacked. In fact quite the opposite. We had to suck up to them in order to receive good treatment. They often tormented me. When I felt unhappy or needed to hide I came here.' He shook his head at the memory of the boy whose eccentric, awkward behaviour had provoked such ill will.

After Japan's surrender in 1945 Mr Abe had returned to the villa. He had nowhere else to go. Everyone feared terrible cruelties from the invading Americans. He thought he might at least find something to eat in his old home. 'We were all starving then.' He had arrived on a hot night in August. The silence struck him first. No maids hurried to the door with shouts of welcome. He had pushed open the shoji screens and wandered from tatami room to tatami room, the mats worn, the shoji screens torn and dusty. Finally an old woman had appeared. Everybody had gone, she said. Only she and the dog remained. Rheumatism and age had kept her there. She looked at the dirt and shrugged. It was too hot for housekeeping she said. He stayed until the autumn. He remembered lying in his bedroom above the Western room wondering if the Americans would come and what they would do to him. The old woman slept in the hall across the front door and the dog in the kitchen. 'It was a strange feeling to be alone in that house. I liked it better.'

I asked if he had learnt falconry as a child. 'Not at all,' said Mr Abe. He had taken it up as a hobby in late middle age. 'It is to get me out of the house. Japanese women don't like their men at home all day.'

On our return Midori was waiting for us in great excitement. Charlie had invited her to Wiltshire to meet his parents. What did one wear over a hunting weekend? I said nothing that looked new. Her face dropped. The wardrobe of a middle-class Japanese woman only contains new clothes. I tried to explain the inverted snobbery of the British upper classes. Midori looked more and more perplexed.

'Above all don't be submissive. Stand up for yourself, especially to his mother.'

'But I must be polite,' said Midori tentatively. 'I must show respect.'

'Only to the housekeeper,' I corrected.

Midori looked so unhappy that I asked if this meant that she and Charlie were getting engaged. 'Well, he hasn't actually said . . . but don't you think . . . is it not a strange thing to do?' I agreed it was. We allowed ourselves to daydream of Midori married to Charlie and living in London. Then she returned to his mother. 'I'm sure we will have many things to talk about. Her family have lived and traded in China for generations.'

'Hong Kong,' I corrected.

'But she has experience of the Far East,' persisted Midori.

'It's not quite the same,' I said unwilling to blot her happiness while trying to imagine the reaction of Charlie's mother to the prospect of a daughter-in-law not only Japanese but five years older than her son.

6

One morning at the Kobokan I found Mr Sato bent over an English song book. He asked me to choose something for the old people. Greensleeves caught my attention. I stood up in front of everybody to explain that this was a love song written by an English king to his mistress. I then described Henry VIII's marital history. This got me into difficulties. I knew how to say 'divorce' in Japanese but I had to mime 'execution' and employ the Japanese word for 'sweetheart' to explain Anne Boleyn and Catherine Howard's adulterous affairs. The old people were charmed, the old ladies by Anne Boleyn's boyfriend, the old men by Henry VIII's novel methods of divorce. Afterwards they sang Greensleeves with gusto. An old man leaned over and said, 'I still don't understand. Why did he have to marry them all?'

Before I left, Mrs Goto asked me to give an English lesson every week. She did not expect the old people to actually study English. She just wanted me to talk about England. I had only ever made one speech in my life and that at least had been in English. I feared this would be as much a failure as the menus and the *oshibori*.

When the calligrapher, Mrs Yamada, finally came to tea she was surprised to be asked about her work. 'Usually I only discuss it with my teacher.' She explained that she practised and practised until the various strokes were not just faultless but part of herself. She spread a large sheet of paper on the tatami mat, knelt down and breathed deeply until she attained 'the right frame of mind'. Then she gathered the ink on to her brush and exploded into action. There was, of course, no touching up afterwards. Either the finished character was perfect or it was not. She showed me two photographs of her work, both of the character for night. One conjured up a soft and balmy evening, 'good for lovers', said Mrs Yamada; the other a menacing, black night. 'I thought of Macbeth and the witches. One of my friends has just translated Shakespeare into Japanese so it was very much in my head.'

All the time she perched on my sofa exquisite in kimono, almost a work of art in herself and the antithesis of the Western idea of the artist. National costume reveals a great deal about a nation's sexual preferences. This is the costume, after all, that has evolved to attract the male population of a particular country over the centuries. The kimono appears the exception. Its severity seems to disdain sexuality. It reduces a woman's curves to straight lines or hides them completely. As I watched Mrs Yamada nibble at some shortbread, the contradictions of the garment over-whelmed me.

A glimpse of the folds of the inner kimono at her throat teased the mind like layers of tissue around a small and expensive gift. The cord around the *obi*, a stiff band of material encompassing the waist, promised release with its undoing into that silky softness. Mrs Yamada raised her hand and patted the back of her chignon. The choice of the nape of the neck as the erogenous zone is so civilized compared to exposed legs and bosoms but at the same time invites images of brutality: a man holding a woman down, biting the back of her neck to ensure compliance and copulation as violent and as fast as an animal's. The very purity and restraint of the garment seemed deliberately designed to excite the beast in the Japanese male. Mrs Yamada finished her biscuit, dabbed her lips and reached for her brocade handbag. Would I like a peanut? She had picked up a packet on the way. They were quite fresh, she believed.

At the Kobokan I had joined the handicraft class which took place once a month. About ten old ladies and I were sitting around a table making rabbits from *oshibori*. We wrapped twine at each end then stuffed the rag ingeniously back into itself to form the body, tail, ears and head. We sewed on the mouth and eyes and brushed the inside of the ears with rouge to give them the requisite pink tinge. There was a lot of arguing and competition amongst the old ladies on how to get their rabbits rabbit-shaped. When not fighting over cotton and buttons they gossiped about that perennially popular subject, their daughters-in-law.

Young women were just not made of the same sturdy stuff as themselves, they agreed, and it affected society. Mrs Goto pointed to Mrs Fujikawa as the type of old-fashioned Japanese woman who held the community together. Small with large, moist eyes and an affection for crocheted jerseys, Mrs Fujikawa had been the wife of a school master and head of the local women's association. She organized food and drink for weddings and funerals. She rounded up neighbours for fire drill and earthquake practice and taught them to carry buckets of water 'the right way'. During the school holidays she stood outside the station handing out leaflets to parents. Mrs Komita explained, 'Boys will hang around in fine weather and pick up the wrong friends. Our leaflets say, "Please watch your son and check his companions!"' As head of the women's association she attended district meetings. 'Of course she's the only woman there so she spends most of the time making tea for the men,' said Mrs Komita.

Everyone agreed Mrs Fujikawa typified the good neighbourliness people associated with the district. 'In this area we support each other,' said Mrs Komita. For example not many possessed a bath. People were always dropping in to use Mrs Fujikawa's, 'sometimes complete strangers', added Mrs Komita. Others appreciated Mrs Fujikawa's cooking. 'She always prepares extra and gives it to her neighbours,' said Mrs Goto.

Many of the old people belonged to the club of the 'Ten Thousand Paces' which Mrs Fujikawa had started after a doctor advised her to take up walking to lower her blood sugar. Every morning she counted out ten thousand paces before performing ten minutes of callisthenics in the park. She finished with a little rubbish collection or leaf sweeping. Mrs Fujikawa was in her eighties.

Throughout the conversation Mrs Fujikawa remained silent. Occasionally she smiled, shook her head at a compliment or protested, 'I don't know about that,' or, more daringly, 'Really, I do nothing out of the ordinary.' Mrs Goto pointed out that few of the new generation followed Mrs Fujikawa's example. They had a job and no time for neighbourhood associations. Said one old lady, 'Now the company takes care of them but what will happen when they retire? How will they fit back into the community?' All the old people saw a lack of neighbourly concern as part of a moral decline in young mothers. Mrs Komita said, 'When my daughter-in-law ticks off her child she never gives him a reason. She just says, "Don't do that because everyone is watching!"' It was not all their fault, remarked Mrs Goto. As adolescents they had to study so hard. They only saw their parents for half an hour every day. Who could learn morality in half an hour? They certainly did not learn it from books! Another old woman shook her head and explained that everyone spoilt their children in the 1950s. The others agreed. Mrs Goto put it down to, 'our imperfect understanding of democracy'. I wondered at the self-sacrifice that this safe, kindly society of the old people's memory had demanded. I enjoyed what Mrs Fujikawa had created but, like the maligned daughters-in-law, I had no intention of emulating her life.

By now various shaped rabbits were emerging from arthritic hands. I held up my soft toy proudly. Mrs Komita looked hard at the head. 'It's all wrong,' she announced to the room in general. 'Why is her rabbit's head a different shape?' We lined up our rabbits and stared at them, Mrs Komita pointed to her own. 'See, it's got a small nose but look at this one,' she tweaked my rabbit. 'Harriet has given her bunny a foreign snout. Look it sticks right out just like her own nose!'

Mrs Yamada, the calligrapher, also demonstrated that a definition of Japanese womanhood was not as simple as the old ladies believed – perhaps it never had been. Tripping down the street in winter kimono and a fur stole, Mrs Yamada certainly looked the part. No one would have guessed that this exquisite apparition enjoyed a passion for peanuts or produced volcanic works of art.

She confused me further when she invited me to an exhibition of her students' work in her home town two hours from Tokyo. She also asked the Ethiopian with whom I had first met her. Her students and their families had never encountered a foreigner before much less an Ethiopian. Mrs Yamada appeared serenely unaware of the sensation we were causing. She introduced us to her father, a tall, old gentleman dressed as traditionally as herself in black kimono over wide, grey, pleated pants or *hakama*. An ivory tobacco pouch intricately carved hung on a cord across his stomach. After this it was with some surprise that I opened the door a month later to find Mrs Yamada in a tee-shirt and slacks. The tee-shirt featured a plastic pouch over the bosom containing a dollar bill and the instructions in red letters to 'Smash and Grab'. Mrs Yamada gave a nervous laugh when I commented on her change of garment. 'More cheerful don't you think,' was all she said. Only as she was departing did she give the reason for her unexpected visit: she had decided to leave her husband.

Divorce is rare in Japan and I had not expected it from Mrs Yamada. When she invited me to her home a week later I went with alacrity. She lived near the Sumida river with her husband who was ten years older than her and an assistant professor at medical university. Their flat consisted of one room in which I could not have comfortably lain down, a galley kitchen, a minute bathroom and a study. It was here that Mrs Yamada did her work. Out of the window stretched a Tokyo cityscape of grey and smoky pink buildings under the pink sky of early evening. In the block of flats opposite a woman was spreading out futons for her children. Across the sky helicopters ferried businessmen home from the golf courses.

We knelt at the table and Mrs Yamada made coffee. She wore a drab dress. Her skin had lost the translucence of her kimono days. She had discovered that her husband had kept a mistress for eleven years by whom he had a daughter now aged eight. 'We never had children of our own,' she said. It was the daughter who had led to the discovery. The courts had sent an order requiring that he pay for her upkeep and Mrs Yamada had opened the letter by mistake. Straightaway she had decided on a divorce. Did her friends agree with the decision, I asked. Of course, she said. Again and again I had been told that Japanese women view marriage as a contract. Yet here was a woman appalled because her husband had taken a mistress. Like so many Japanese women, she said one thing while expecting something better. She had decided she did not want a row. She merely told her husband to sort the matter out. 'It's your business,' she said.

Mrs Yamada explained that her husband was a proud, old-fashioned man. As a professor he commanded respect. 'Maybe he had too much his own way,' she admitted. When he procrastinated, no doubt hoping his wife would calm down, she took the extraordinary step of making an appointment with a lawyer and forcing him to keep it. In the lawyer's office he sat straight backed, his face rigid with shock. She explained why she wanted a divorce. Finally he was forced to speak. Without looking at his wife, he said that he had decided to leave his mistress but, at the age of forty, she had become pregnant. It was the first time and she wanted to keep the child. They never had a proper financial arrangement. He gave her money when she asked for it. He did not know how much that had come to over the years.

Afterwards, 'as if nothing had happened', exclaimed Mrs Yamada indignantly, he returned home with her, sat down at the table and looked expectant. 'He was waiting for his dinner just as normal. Of course I had nothing prepared. I assumed he would go to a hotel.' Mrs Yamada pressed a tissue to her lips and shook her head.

The next morning he asked her 'breakfast?' She said 'no breakfast today'. He replied 'Ah so,' and went to work. That afternoon he collapsed with a cerebral haemorrhage. At the hospital they told his wife that he could barely move and certainly would never be able to look after himself again. Mrs Yamada wasted no time on emotion. She saw immediately the consequences. He had trapped her more surely than if he had refused a divorce. I wondered at the intensity of his passion and disbelief, the shock, almost enough to kill him, of revealing his secret to his wife and the lawyer. Mrs Yamada had little patience for such speculation. She now found herself visiting the hospital twice a day. Japanese nurses are in short supply and Japanese hospitals rely on the female relatives of patients to provide care. Many of my middle-aged women friends got their children into university (a full-time occupation for a woman in Japan), only to find their days and nights taken up nursing parents and in-laws. Mrs Yamada stayed in the hospital five or six hours a day. 'I have an exhibition coming soon,' she said. 'I try and work at night but I am so tired.'

She had to take in food, turn him, wash him, then change his dirty pyjamas, take them home and wash them. The intimacy of it appalled her. I suggested she set up a rota with his sisters and even demand that the mistress take a turn. She smiled then shook her head. She did not want either his family or the doctors and nurses at the hospital to know about her husband's affair. As a professor, they respected him. The arrival of a strange woman would cause them 'to lose their admiration and his care would suffer'.

She then offered to sell one of her paintings to me. I had assumed the chance to buy her work would only come after years of friendship, but now she needed the money. The hospital cost a great deal and the mistress was still demanding contributions for the child. I got up to go. At the door she said, 'My friends think I ought to have suspected something. We weren't exactly happy, I suppose, but life was tranquil. I thought that was enough.'

A few days later Mrs Yamada rang up and asked me to accompany her father to a poetry reading. She could not go herself as she had to nurse her husband, 'but my father has come especially to Tokyo for the event.' I met him on a street corner. At first I did not recognize the old man. He had exchanged his kimono for a Western suit and it appeared to have shrunk him. Stress and

113

bewilderment replaced the calm expression he had worn in the countryside.

We took a train to Tokyo's business district. Mrs Yamada's father led me to an old wooden house slumped between two skyscrapers overlooking a railway line. The ground floor contained a restaurant serving Japanese country food. Waiters with red head bands shouted orders from the customers seated around a wooden counter. The father of the owner had transported the house from the countryside to the centre of Tokyo. The owner himself enjoyed poetry and let poets use an upstairs floor for meetings.

Mrs Yamada's father, visibly expanding in the rural atmosphere of the place, led me up steps as narrow and steep as a ladder to a private room half covered in tatami mats. At the centre of the mats lay an open fire over which hung a cooking pot from a hook decorated with a wooden carp. Around the pot sat Japan's most eminent poets. In the place of honour, seated cross-legged, was the Croatian poet whose work I had seen the week before in the *Herald Tribune*. I had assumed he gave readings in concert halls. 'Do all foreign poets come here?' I asked Mrs Yamada's father. 'There's nowhere else,' he said. We stepped over the shoes that cluttered up the entrance and nudged ourselves into a place beside the cooking pot.

The Croatian's poetry was read three times in three different languages; first with great *élan* by the writer in Serbo-Croat, then timidly in Japanese, and last pedantically by an earnest American girl. At eight o'clock a small and venerable Japanese stood up to interrupt. He apologized to the poet, 'but many of us have started to think of our dinner.' The owner of the restaurant entered carrying not the usual minute portions of Japanese food but platters of stuffed fish and vegetables. I found myself next to the person whom the earnest American girl had described as Japan's foremost poet. Tall and cadaverous with very white skin, he refused the food. The dishes, he complained, were too heavy to lift. This meant I ate equally little as he declined to pass me anything. He and the Croatian poet discussed the various poetry

114

symposia they had attended. They recalled Rome, Toronto and Barcelona rather as businessmen recollecting conferences or soldiers their campaigns. In Barcelona the Japanese poet had got carried away and married a South American writer. He implied this had not been altogether successful. 'She is very exhausting,' he said.

After the meal, the venerable Japanese made a speech praising and thanking the restaurant owner then introducing everyone around the pot. Poetry appeared the qualification for the evening. The older, male poets smiled benignly on young women who announced themselves as mere writers. I took a mouthful of tofu and described myself as 'an eating person'.

The venerable man and I exchanged name cards. He taught English literature at one of Japan's leading universities. The British National Theatre had just visited Tokyo with two productions. I asked if he had enjoyed them. He waved dismissively. 'I sent my students,' he said. Had he not wanted to go himself, I pursued. He looked taken aback. 'I saw Olivier's films so I don't need to see another Shakespeare production,' he said firmly. I pointed out that Western theatrical tradition depended on fresh interpretations of plays. He looked at me as if I was mad. 'There is only one interpretation of Shakespeare and that is Olivier's,' he reiterated. I began to argue but his face took on the closed expression Japanese assume when assailed by Western logic. He knew better. He had taught the West's greatest playwright for thirty years in the approved Japanese way. He was the teacher and his the only opinion that mattered. Here, I thought, sat one of the Bard's few failures. Years of immersion in Shakespeare had made no impression on this pedantic soul.

He leaned across me and asked Japan's leading poet to recite. Everyone joined in. The Japanese poet shook his head and explained that he was much too shy. Finally he agreed but on one condition. He insisted that his friend accompany him. The friend, a handsome and ebullient man with a moustache, proved to be one of the Ainu, an ethnic people living in the far north of the country, noted for their hairiness. When the poet began, the Ainu

115

burst into a howl and howled so loudly and ferociously that none of us could hear Japan's most eminent poet. Safely drowned in howls, the poet finished and sat down again smiling benignly at his audience.

Mrs Yamada's decision to divorce represented an intimation of change in Japanese society. I discovered this for myself when Mr Sato asked me to speak about my impressions of Japanese society at a conference on 'Internationalism'. After reading my first draft he frowned. 'Please, I want you to say something from your heart,' he said, touching his own and screwing up his face. 'I may not be polite about Japan,' I warned. Mr Sato beamed. 'All the better,' he said. Mr Sato, I realized, wanted to make use of me. As a foreigner I could say things no Japanese would dare articulate.

The conference took place in the expensive new Sumida-ku Community Centre. In the past, Tokyo's city councils shunned the workshops and junkets considered necessary by their British counterparts. They provided pot plants for new mothers or the occasional bag of leaf mould for pensioners. Only recently has civic activism become fashionable. Sumida-ku celebrated the trend by building itself the sort of headquarters where even the ladies lavatory glistened with white marble. It was an incongruous landmark in the city's poorest district.

The conference revealed a typically Japanese interpretation of internationalism. The Japanese were fascinated by what foreigners thought of them. The audience listened enthralled to my criticism of Japanese society. 'She's so severe,' they murmured rapturously. They were, however, less interested in foreigners themselves. The two Japanese speakers who had performed good works abroad received scant attention. Most of all the audience saw internation-alism as an engine of change at home. One by one ordinary men and women of all ages who had come out on a cold and rainy Sunday stood up and called for the transformation of this most conservative of societies. They discussed taboo subjects: Japanese atrocities during the Second World War and the mistreatment of Koreans who have lived in Japan for three or four generations.

116

Just as I wondered if political correctness had finally reached Japan, an old man rose to his feet. He was deaf and dumb. The Japanese usually hide away their handicapped but, in the new spirit of internationalism, the conference organizers had invited a group of deaf mutes together with translators. The old man hitched up his trousers, then exploded into sign language. He whacked his head, hit his cheeks, clapped his hands and screwed up his fingers. Translation appeared superfluous. 'If the Koreans don't like it here, why don't they go back to Korea. And why should we apologize for the War?' he added in a final outburst of slapping. An awful silence fell upon the hall. Here was every liberal's worst nightmare: one minority attacking another. Suddenly a Korean woman erupted from the audience and stormed up the aisle. In rapid, gunfire Japanese she splattered the audience with a history of Japanese atrocities.

I asked my neighbour to translate. He looked first dazed then embarrassed. He pulled himself together and said resolutely, 'Impossible — she is talking much too fast. We Japanese can't understand a word that she is saying,' and he stared ahead. Internationalism, in Sumida-ku, had its limits.

Midori's own efforts at internationalism proved even less successful. She returned from England downcast. Despite coming from a family which had made its fortune out of the Far East, Charlie's mother refused to meet Midori or allow her inside the house. Charlie took her to stay with his uncle and aunt instead. Nor had anything she had learnt from me prepared Midori for the shock of the English countryside.

Tokyoites such as Midori hold firm views about the countryside. They enjoy it best from the hermetically sealed window of a luxury hotel. When they do venture out it is to a gift shop, more common than paddy fields in rural Japan, or on to a golf course. They dress impeccably, the men in blazers, the women in high-heeled shoes with white as the preferred colour. So it was with increasing rage and incomprehension that Midori attempted to trip over the ploughed fields of Wiltshire. She had never heard of gumboots before, let alone the concept of going for a walk. 'I was always expecting to get somewhere,' she moaned. 'I kept on asking when are we going to get there. Please tell me, why do people walk for no reason and in old clothes?'

The evenings equally unnerved her. She dismissed Charlie's female relatives as overweight and badly dressed. She said, 'I felt sorry for his cousins. Who is going to marry them?' Then she overheard them complaining to Charlie that she 'tried too hard' and looked overdone, 'like a shop girl'. As Midori considered the hour she spent every day on her appearance a virtue, the contempt of this remark escaped her. She marvelled at their confidence. They joined in arguments and interrupted the men. They talked all the time about people Midori did not know or parties she had not attended. 'They never asked me about myself. I just sat there nodding my head and smiling. I felt so stupid.'

'That was the idea,' I said.

'You always say we Japanese are so rude,' said Midori reproachfully, 'but really, aren't the English worse?'

She grumbled about the cold. 'Charlie's family is quite rich I think but they have no central heating except in the corridors. What do English people do in the corridors all winter?' Midori had borrowed a blow heater from the maid's room which she kept on day and night. The unaccustomed warmth had woken a wasp hibernating in the curtains which promptly stung her. She had rushed out of her room only to find Charlie's uncle seated there calmly polishing the family's shoes. This sight so staggered Midori that she forgot about the wasp sting. 'I thought maybe he suffers from some kind of foot fetish,' she confided. I explained that men who had been to public school and in the army frequently got out the shoe box on a Sunday evening. Midori remained sceptical. 'Well I kept my shoes locked up after that. I did not want them molested.'

The visit came to an end when Charlie caught his aunt ringing his mother with an account of Midori's antics. She had been doing so every night since the couple's arrival. The behaviour of his family had an inflammatory effect on Charlie. He announced his

118

engagement to Midori and threw a party on their return to Tokyo. Later he told me that he planned to buy a plot of land and build a house outside Tokyo from the profits he had made as a broker. He explained to me, 'I want her to have a home here. When we move to London it's important she owns something in Japan. It will make her happy.'

I wondered if Charlie did not view this acquisition of land as a means of firming his resolve. Charlie exuded something soft and catlike. It was part of his charm. His indolence provoked a reaction in strong women. They felt they only had to seize him by the scruff of his neck and dump him in their lap for all that warm, purring pleasure to be their own. The threat lurked, however, that he would escape as easily as he had been acquired. Charlie loved Midori. She offered him the chance to elude his own weakness and the slow death he foresaw on a return to England and his family. He wanted to stay with her. In a moment of insight he had decided an investment in land a more binding proposition than marriage or even love.

Charlie explained all this to me in a Ginza hostess bar. He had taken me there when I had asked to meet one of Tokyo's top *mama-sans*. At six o'clock on a cold evening in the Ginza, Tokyo's smartest and most expensive nightclub and shopping district, hostesses in fur jackets hurried from the hairdressers towards the bars. In the coffee shops, hostess-bar managers, the men behind the *mama-sans* known as *kurofuku* or 'men in black suits', sipped Russian tea and made secret deals. Out on the street corner the ricecake seller set up his stall for the drunken salary men who in a few hours time would want something hot to nibble as they waited for a taxi home.

Ginza nightlife revolves around the *mama-san*, the female owner or manager of a bar. A bar's popularity rises or falls on her personality. In the most exclusive, a man pays £500 for a drink and a chat. Salary men stay at their desks until midnight each evening enticed by the reward, as a future company president, of entry to such establishments and the chance to be fussed over by

Japan's most experienced *mama-sans*. In need of a little spoiling myself, I set out to discover what a man gets, as the bill states, for 'charm charge'.

A few hours drinking in a Ginza bar was a serious financial proposition. Mr Ogawa, a friend of Charlie's, worked for a foreign trading company and promoted the company's products by ordering champagne and brandy in Ginza bars. He owed Charlie a favour and so one evening took us with him. We made our way around a number of establishments, ending up in Mr Ogawa's favourite and the most expensive. By then I had learnt to guess the size of the bill by the number of steps it took to get from the door to one's seat. The cheapest required only a shuffle and an apology. This bar allowed a leisurely promenade past a grand piano and a gigantic vase of orchids. Dotted about the room elegant young hostesses chatted to politicians and the heads of Japan's leading companies. I was the only woman there not a hostess.

The *mama-san* hurried over to us, three girls in tow. Mr Ogawa, an experienced campaigner of Ginza nightlife, was an old friend. The *mama-san* sat herself between us, an exquisite creature in kimono, her hair drawn back in a chignon fixed with a gold pin. She immediately started making jokes and ordering drinks, her energy and enthusiasm wrapping us up and launching us into a night of pleasure like a strong wind. Mr Ogawa ordered a bottle of Dom Perignon. The *mama-san* broke into a smile of such spontaneous pleasure that she forgot to cover her mouth with her hand and hide her bad teeth.

I asked to what she attributed her success as one of the Ginza's most celebrated *mama-sans*. 'Sincerity,' she replied breaking into peals of laughter. What would she do on retirement? I asked. 'That's not the sort of question to ask in a hostess bar,' said Mr Ogawa firmly. The *mama-san* looked relieved. She did not care to spoil the carefully created atmosphere with replies that drew attention away from the men and on to herself. Instead she introduced me to a girl in a slip of expensive black silk who confessed her favourite designer was Valentino. (Most Japanese women refuse to wear Valentino now because it is so popular with hostesses.) Out of a monthly salary of ¥700,000 (£4,200) she spent ¥450,000 (£2,700) on clothes for a 'total fashion look' she assured me, including underwear and accessories. 'Bad girl, don't you save?' teased Mr Ogawa. 'Well, I never eat,' she replied. 'If you take me out to dinner, I am quite happy with a bowl of noodles!' The jokes snapped back and forth between him and the women. He accused them of buttering him up. The *mama-san* protested hard. 'She thinks buttering up means to make a fool of,' Mr Ogawa translated blandly for me.

We left on a wave of good feeling. Five hostesses and the *mama-san* put us into the lift and bowed as the doors closed. Young men (added to the bill as 'boy charge' as opposed to the hostesses who appear as 'charm charge') escorted us tenderly to our car. I lay back, enchanted. After my initial awkward questions the *mama-san* and I had enjoyed a long conversation. In her mid-thirties, she had appeared a serious and intelligent woman forced into a job she disliked because Japanese society had failed to offer an alternative. In the United Kingdom she may have run her own company. That she thought I looked like an actress out of *Dangerous Liaisons* only increased my conviction that here was a remarkable woman.

When I rang to see her again her reaction proved somewhat different. At first she did not remember me. Then she said, 'What's the point?' Finally, she agreed to have supper with me.

She arrived fresh from the hairdresser in a kimono of pearly silk that glimmered in the gloom of the restaurant. Her skin had an almost translucent quality which, the more I heard of the rigours of her job, seemed increasingly miraculous. She had grown up in a small town, the daughter of a working-class family. After a brief marriage she had started work in the Ginza. Long-term business for the bar depended on her becoming a customer's friend. That meant sending a card on a customer's birthday or telephoning, during unusually hot or cold weather, to check he was well. Sometimes customers invited her to play golf. She would wake at six in the morning, after getting to bed only three hours before, play all day then, pausing only for a brief visit to the hairdresser, go straight to work. When not playing golf she spent the day telephoning. She kept a record of every customer's visit. Those who had not come for some time, she chased up. 'Some girls are not so diligent. They spend all their time in health clubs,' she added, disapprovingly.

The club only welcomed new customers with a proper introduction. She followed up good prospects, such as lawyers, doctors or presidents of middle-sized or large companies, the next day with a telephone call urging them to come again soon. During quiet months she invited clients to dinner before taking them to the club. They always paid. She ordered another whisky and water, her third in half an hour. She had not eaten anything. I asked with how many men she had cultivated this special relationship. 'Goodness me, I could not possibly count, hundreds perhaps.' Opposite us, a middle-aged *mama-san* in kimono sat rigidly straight, picking at her food while her male companion slumped back, legs apart, tie loosened.

The harsh financial set up of the clubs dictated her behaviour. She lacked, it emerged, the independence I had attributed to her class. The risks all fell on her and the hostesses rather than the owner, usually a gangster. Like everything else in Japan, the clubs work on a strictly hierarchical system. A girl started as help and was paid by the night, usually about ¥30,000 (£180). If enough customers found her charming, she approached another club, promising to deliver her customers to them. At the new club she became a contractual hostess, her earnings based on how much her customers ate and drank. The *mama-san* could not introduce a hostess's customers to another hostess, only to the help. The help could only make money from a customer if she moved bars which meant a continual turnover. Every year both *mama-san* and hostess stated how much they proposed to earn for the club. If they failed to meet their target after ten months, they had to pay the difference and leave. Towards the end of that period customers found hostesses ready to offer any inducement if they would come to the bar and help fulfil the girl's quota. 'That's why hostesses have a bad reputation,' said the *mama-san*. If a customer failed to pay his bill after two months, his hostess had to pay it herself. 'It's a very severe business,' admitted the *mama-san*.

The *mama-san* had as much responsibility as any middle manager but no power. She could not hire or fire hostesses or even alter the decor of the club. 'Ginza is a conservative place. It's impossible to change the system. The club never fails to make money whatever happens to us.' I asked why she wore kimono. 'I have got fat,' she admitted. Unable to compete against the slim young hostesses, she had retreated into the elegance of kimono. What would she do in the future, I asked. Now she earned ten million yen a year (£60,000) plus a percentage of the turnover but at thirty-five, however beautiful, her time was limited. Would she open her own bar? The *mama-san* looked uncomfortable. It was all terribly expensive. She did not relish the responsibility; she was, like most Japanese, an employee, but without a job for life or a pension. Marriage did not appear an option either. Japanese men disliked wives skilled in *ichatsuku* or 'chat up'. (Japanese does not have a word for flirt.) That was why she had agreed to meet me. What about a foreign husband? She had heard they were very amenable.

Here was another myth exploded. I had expected to meet the legendary *mama-san*, strong-willed and independent, a cross between barmaid and Madam. Instead she was in thrall to a system that suppressed individuality and, apart from an extraordinary ability to flatter, her mind was as pedestrian as her job. Midori offered to introduce me to a friend of hers who ran her own bar. 'She's certainly independent,' said Midori. We met in the Ginza. For some time we walked about in the cold because Midori had lost the bar. 'I am sure it was here,' she said as we turned around and started again. I did not remonstrate. A hint of impatience, or even an impersonal remark on the weather would have mortified a Japanese friend. We found the bar eventually. A row of office buildings concealed the entrance to a minute alleyway. At the end, partially obscured by the gloom, rose a flight of steep and narrow steps. Midori walked up first and opened a door into a room the size of the average bathroom. It contained enough space for the bar and one table. Three customers, all men, sat around drinking.

The owner was middle aged, wore a fake Chanel suit and exuded the air of a really efficient secretary. She had worked in an office until the age of thirty-two. Despite ability and dedication the company blocked her promotion. Instead they hinted that she ought to marry. When she refused they pointed out that she was getting too old 'to adorn the office'. She should make way for a younger face. Finally they asked her to leave. She said, 'I decided the only way to get on was to start on my own.'

Here also her options were limited. After some research she decided a bar offered the best chance of independence. She did not bother to go to a bank for a loan – 'they would have turned me down' – but used her savings and asked her father for help. 'He wanted me to stand on my own two feet but thought running my own bar too ambitious, especially in the Ginza where there is so much competition.'

On the shelf behind stretched ten feet of whisky bottles each labelled with the name of a regular customer. Midori mentioned a mutual friend and the bar owner took down his whisky bottle and poured us a drink. 'He'd want you to have some,' she said cheerfully. One of the customers announced, 'This bar's the most popular in the area. It's exactly what a salary man needs when its you that's paying and not the company. You don't have to worry about the price, it's always the same.' The bar owner explained that she charged a fixed price which had not changed for ten years. It included the dish of the day the mention of which made Midori laugh and point to the stove. 'We always see a pot there but never anything in it.' The bar owner shrugged. She wanted to cut costs so she just did one dish that was 'easy to prepare'. She employed no one else. When she fell ill or went on holiday, the bar closed. She did not spend money on her hair or clothes. 'Sex appeal is not part of my repertoire,' she added, fingering the bow at her throat. She teased her customers and they teased her. Men wanted somewhere apart from their home and their office where they could relax. 'How can you relax in a one-roomed apartment with a two and a four year old?' she added. Men were always on the look out for a cheap bar. 'Mine fits the bill.'

When she started, 'I was a real innocent.' She did not even know how to register a bar. Colleagues from her old company took her on a bar crawl to teach her the business. These colleagues became her first customers. Then she enjoyed a friendship with a *mama-san* in Osaka. When the *mama-san*'s regulars moved to Tokyo, she gave them the bar owner's address. Midori recalled arriving for the first time shortly after the bar opened. The owner nodded. 'I was so shy at the beginning that I never said a word. Some men with dirty minds seeing I was a woman on my own made some pretty crude suggestions.' At first she did not know how to react. 'Then I told them, "It's the cheapest bar in the area and for that price you don't get me as well!" The funny thing is that they understood that and left me alone.'

She earned about ¥50,000 a night which worked out at a million yen (£6,000) a month. 'That's the bottom line. If I can earn a million yen a month I can lead my own life. I was determined to make that much in order to impress my father. He died last spring. I am not really ambitious for more.' Travel proved her one luxury. 'It's how I relax.' Customers caused her the most stress. Was she not bothered by *yakuza* demanding protection money? She started laughing again. 'The bar's too small for them and anyway how could they find it? Look how much difficulty you had and Midori's been coming here for years!' The salary man nodded his head. 'Only regulars come here,' he said emphatically.

The bar owner invited us to a party she was holding in a hotel to celebrate the tenth anniversary of the bar and to thank her customers. 'Very smart,' said Midori when she heard where it was to be. The man next to me who boasted a thick moustache shook his head. He could not attend, he said gloomily, because he had to go on a family skiing holiday. His companions all pulled faces. He did not have any choice, he insisted. His daughters were running wild, one with a Libyan diplomat, the other with a French cook. His wife wanted the family to go on holiday together and sort it out. He looked despondent. 'I don't think it will do much good. I hardly ever see them and I certainly can't control them.' The bar owner said foreigners were not such a bad proposition. 'Look at Midori here. She's got a rich foreign boyfriend.' 'I was rich before,' exclaimed Midori stoutly. The bar owner laughed, 'No no you weren't. You lived in such a small flat when I first knew you that you didn't even need a telephone extension cord!'

We stayed drinking Midori's friend's whisky until two in the morning. Out in the cold night, Midori appeared reluctant to return home and suggested another bar in a basement lined with wood. It offered every kind of whisky. Midori looked around nostalgically. She said, 'I used to meet a man here years ago. He was a famous television presenter but married. He didn't want one of the weeklies to report our affair so we came to this place.' She sat without speaking, sipping the malt. I wondered at this other existence, barely referred to with her foreign friends. Did she still see her Japanese friends, I asked. She replied, 'Charlie doesn't like them phoning the apartment.' Like many foreign men he had found it all too easy to adopt the domineering demeanour of the typical Japanese male. I gave her a lecture on self-reliance. 'Like my bar lady friend?' she said with a smile. 'That kind of woman doesn't get very far in Japan.' She paid the bill and we left.

My friendship with Midori, like my time at the Kobokan, had thrust me into a very different Japan to the one I had entered with such distress on my arrival. The success of these relationships overspilled into every aspect of my life. I saw everything Japanese, even Mrs Abe, in an optimistic light. I had entered an irritating phase common to most foreigners. My host country could do no wrong. I had found a blessed place where the natives were forever smiling. I was at the high point of my immersion into Japan.

It was in this mood that I made friends with Dolly Kurata. She had arrived in Japan in 1920, married a Japanese and lived in the country ever since. Nothing, not even the Second World War, had dented her enthusiasm for the Japanese. A small English-woman in her nineties with large blue eyes, she invariably wore a big hat and loose, stylish clothes. She invited me to tea with her friend, another Englishwoman married to a Japanese. Betty had left England in the 1950s but still retained the air of a county lady more at home organizing tennis parties than being married to the 'second son' of a wealthy Japanese family and life as 'second wife' in the family compound. 'Second son' sat meekly at her side.

Dolly was a widow. She pulled out photographs of her early married life which revealed a stunning creature in playful, seductive poses at her husband's side. My conversation on the erotic adventures of foreigners in Shanghai between the wars had fired up the old ladies. Both talked loudly over the other. They were particularly taken by the phrase 'sexual harassment'. Dolly described fifty years of sexual harassment over a number of continents. 'The British were the worst. One man thrust his leg between mine on the top of a double decker bus. Well,' she said sadly, 'I suppose that's all over now.'

Despite spending their entire adult lives in the country, Betty could not speak Japanese while Dolly employed a pigeon version only. Betty was discussing the recent newspaper accounts of Japanese husbands henpecked by their wives. She dismissed these as 'quite ridiculous!', then watched in exasperation as her husband began to fumble in his pocket. Finally he pulled out a *meishi* (name card) which he presented to me. 'Take no notice,' said Betty, waving it away. 'It's a reflex action. He can't help himself.'

After this I often met Dolly at the Press Club for lunch. She had come to Japan to join her brother who was working for Reuters in Tokyo. He was transferred to Shanghai. She stayed on in Tokyo living in a boarding house run by White Russians. Japan, 'with its narrow streets, low houses and everyone in kimono', had instantly captivated her.

She took a job at Reuters and plunged into Japanese life. When her Japanese colleagues invited her to kabuki theatre or sushi bars, the British community accused her of 'going native'. 'So I didn't have anything more to do with my fellow countrymen,' announced Dolly. She met her future husband on a picnic arranged by her secretary. He was, in fact, her secretary's brother

127

who was studying to pass the Japanese Foreign Office exams. He already spoke English and Spanish. They fell in love immediately or, as Dolly put it, 'reached an understanding'. A few months later he was sent to Mexico. Dolly lived with the family until his departure. The father, a descendant of a samurai, had studied law in America and become a Methodist. After an encounter with a blind beggar playing the flute in the snow, he spent his inheritance setting up a school for the blind. The family were 'as poor as church mice', only supported by the sister's secretarial job.

When he left – 'I knew I would marry no other man but he had problems and I did not want to push him' – Dolly moved to Paris where she worked for an American bank. I remarked that Paris must have been fascinating in the 1920s, but she replied crisply, 'Only if you were an American. They were buying up everything. We all hated the rich, spoilt Yankees.' She did not think much of America generally, I was to discover. After five years she transferred to New York. She and the Japanese diplomat had barely communicated in that time. Once in Manhattan she dispatched a telegram reading, 'At least now we are on the same side of the ocean.' This did the trick. He took the next train up from Mexico. She caught a taxi to Grand Central station. The traffic was terrible. She arrived at the station late. 'He was already walking towards the exit. What would have happened if I had got there five minutes later? We would never have found each other again.'

After marriage and the inclusion of her name on the family register, they lived in Mexico, then Seville where her two children were born. In 1938 she moved back to Japan. Her husband planned to follow but war broke out. She found herself alone in Japan with two children. She looked at me belligerently. Even a brief acquaintanceship with Dolly Kurata made me pause here. 'I don't want to hear a lot of nonsense about Japanese cruelty and aggression,' she warned. 'The Japanese behaved with admirable restraint. In the 1930s they bent over backwards to accommodate American demands. But when America tried bullyboy tactics, the Japanese took a stand. The Americans had failed to colonize Japan

128

and they never forgave the Japanese for not becoming another Hawaii.' To this unusual view of history I said not a word.

Dolly went on now trembling with emotion. 'They were wonderful to me during the war, wonderful. The authorities offered me bread and sugar rations because I was a foreigner. No Japanese received them.' She recalled going into a chemist to buy aspirin. The chemist showed her empty shelves. 'Well you've got a lot of nothing,' said Dolly good-humouredly. An old lady waiting behind her bowed and apologized saying, 'We are at war and have to do without. But it is our war not yours and we are sorry you should suffer too.' Dolly paused then said, 'For years I could not tell that story without crying.'

Her neighbour was a woman with a weak heart and a five-year-old child to whom Dolly occasionally gave bread and sugar. 'Every month that woman returned from the countryside carrying a sake bottle full of milk and two pounds of butter for me. All my neighbours brought me back supplies from the countryside because they knew I had no relatives to send me food.' She recalled women seeing their sons or husbands off at the station them coming to her to weep. 'It would have been unpatriotic to break down in front of other Japanese, even their own families. Don't think Japan undertook the war lightly. It caused terrible suffering. Yet even when the Americans were fire-bombing Tokyo, no one said a word against me.' I asked if the Japanese had not let her down once. 'Never,' she said, her eyes watering with conviction. 'They are a wonderful, wonderful people.'

Dolly insisted on paying every time we went out together. Shortly after the American occupation, on which Dolly held a dim view, she had persuaded her husband to spend $1,000 from his pension on a plot of land in central Tokyo. Forty years later she had sold it for thirty million dollars. 'Now I am awash with money,' she said as if it were a pleasant convenience like hot water.

Dolly invited me to a talk given by Japan's most famous pilot in the Second World War. Saburo Sakai had taken part in 200 dogfights and notched up sixty-four kills. He had survived an attack on his plane when despite severe wounds and almost blinded, he had still managed to fly back to base. Now Dolly had decided to take him on. 'He has some very strange ideas about the war,' she said severely.

Mr Sakai was a small man with pendulous ear lobes. Half a century had not diminished the outrage he felt against Japan's 'top brass'. History books of the period shocked him into writing his own. 'The authors are all leaders who exaggerate their successes and hide their failures', or as Mr Sakai more pungently put it, 'cover their arses'. He himself was 'a simple lower-class man' who joined the air force as a non–commissioned officer. It was for the non–commissioned officers and ratings that he produced his nine history books about the Second World War. 'I flunked college but I thought if I can speak, I can write.'

He went on to tell stories of atrocities perpetrated by Japanese commanders against their own men. Most of the audience were made up of elderly Japanese males who sat forward in their seats, listening intently. In a country which keeps silent on the war Mr Sakai was a rare man. He received threats from right-wing extremists because he had singled out and criticized individual commanders. He expected they would refute his claims but they made no response. A number of men from the lower ranks wrote and telephoned to congratulate him. Most added, 'But it's too late now. Does it matter anymore?'

Dolly was deaf so she only caught a part of this. It proved enough to outrage her. At question time she walked purposefully up to the old fighter. They were both barely five feet tall, he seventy-six and she ninety-two. She addressed him in her simple, kitchen Japanese. He, recognizing that he had met his match, pressed her hand, smiled warmly and did not attempt to argue. 'All that talk about atrocities,' she said to me, her eyes snapping with outrage, 'nothing but sob stories!' and, adjusting her hat to an attractive tilt, she marched out.

In the middle of December, the Kobokan announced that it was putting on its annual Nativity play. To get a bit of racial diversity,

130

the Kobokan offered the parts of the wise men to a visiting Filipino social worker called Frank, myself and a Japanese girl. In Sumida-ku, at least, Frank and I represented the exotic.

Mr Sato had written the play from the standpoint of a retired sea captain who owned the stable where Jesus was born. He aimed to appeal to the hard-up families of the neighbourhood. Most had as much idea of Christianity as the Japanese department store which one December displayed Father Christmas nailed to a cross decorated with fairy lights. After the first read-through, Mr Sato asked everyone to learn their lines by the next rehearsal. Unlike the equivalent British production, I assumed they would. Japanese are perfectionists even as amateurs. I practised my one line assiduously.

The rehearsal took place in the Kobokan's gymnasium. In the centre sat Mr Sato on the only chair. The rest of us stood around in costumes made from sheets, one tied Arab fashion on the head. The scenery consisted of a black backdrop, a large tree with transparent leaves and resourceful lighting. The actor playing the lead role of the sea captain, a thick-set man with curly hair, barely knew his part. Nervousness made him inaudible and he kept on stopping to mop his brow. It grew very cold. People put blankets and coats on over their sheets. Mrs Fujikawa who was singing in the choir handed out bags of a jelly-like substance which exuded heat when shaken. I shoved mine down my vest and jumped up and down. Mrs Fujikawa asked kindly who of my family and friends planned to come to the performance. I shook my head. Everybody had refused including my husband and Midori who had gone into peals of laughter. 'But it's the other side of Tokyo, Harriet, fourteen stops on the subway!' Nida had said she might think about it when I told her about Frank. 'He's young and good looking. Bring your sisters,' I entreated. After I returned from one rehearsal blue with cold even she changed her mind.

At the end of the rehearsal, Mr Sato again encouraged the cast to learn their lines adding, 'If you can't, please make them up so no one will know that you have forgotten them.' He then called me aside. I said my line with great impact, 'but perhaps not the

131

right emphasis', he murmured. This I already knew. The entire hall had erupted in laughter. 'It means "the comet has a long tail"' I said. Mr Sato shook his head, 'Well almost, "it has been a long journey" actually,' he corrected as politely as he could. So much, I thought, for a year's Japanese lessons. Perhaps I should not stare quite so intently at the sky, he added. Behind us the chorus broke into Greensleeves. 'That's a love song,' I pointed out to Mr Sato. He waved his hand dismissing 500 years of history. 'It's a carol now,' he said cheerfully.

Before the performance Mr Sato handed me the obligatory sheet to wear, somebody's sewing box to carry and a length of turquoise material which I wound around my head as a turban. 'I am not sure about the pink lipstick,' said Frank, the Filipino. We walked from the back of the hall down the centre aisle to the Japanese version of Deus in Excelsis. As we passed, the audience erupted. Rustling turned to a roar as people jumped up to stare and exclaim at the strange wise men. The children let out high screams of 'Foreigner, foreigner'. Some hid under chairs or in their mothers' laps. The same urge overtook me. I wanted desperately to creep away or merely belong. Frank missed his step getting on to the stage and I forgot the first word of my five-word line. Afterwards I asked Mr Sato for an explanation of the audience's reaction. 'Surely they have seen foreigners before?' Not like you,' said Mr Sato who was very pleased with me. I understood better when he showed me photographs of the event. I had indeed presented an extraordinary sight. The turban increased my height to over six feet and, together with the pink lipstick, made me look like an ageing 1930s Hollywood starlet.

After supper a crowd of boys dressed in starched surplices gathered at the entrance of the Kobokan. They were going carol singing. 'Is this usual for Japan?' I asked. Mr Sato shook his head. Like the Nativity play, the carol singing belonged to the Kobokan's missionary past. Both were rituals unique to the institution. I felt the urge to go with them and discover how Japanese reacted to carols on their doorsteps. In the bitter cold we hurried down alleyways, the choir boys shouting and hitting each other. They stopped abruptly before a small house and burst into Silent Night. An old man in his eighties hobbled out and clapped his hands. He had attended the Kobokan as a child. 'We always stop and sing for him. It cheers him up,' explained Mr Sato. Off we hurried again, Mr Sato on a bicycle, the boys still squabbling. 'This is the underside of Tokyo,' insisted Mr Sato. I remarked that the area looked peaceful enough. 'Drug taking, child abuse and gangsters,' puffed Mr Sato. I asked if they caused him trouble. 'We both want to recruit the same men,' he shrugged and pedalled off before I could question him further.

I caught up with him outside a block of flats typical of the city. Overlooking railway lines and a factory, the heavy steel doors of each apartment resembled prison doors. It provided a desolate scene. The boys gathered in front of the bicycle sheds, tugged at their surplices and started singing Oh Little Town of Bethlehem. A train roared passed. At first nobody seemed interested, then doors began to open and people appeared, leaning on the railings and looking down. Others stood about lighting cigarettes and stamping at the cold. The boys' voices rose into the air, the carol echoing across the wasteland of modern Tokyo. People feel silent, watching the children's faces. It was the closest I had come to experiencing Christianity as a force rather than a ritual. The carol ended, people clapped and the Kobokan choir hooted and scampered off.

A few days later I attended a rather different celebration in Nara, an ancient cultural capital of Japan which boasts a deer park dotted about with Shinto temples. Once a year the priests of a particular temple remove the god from his shrine and take him on an outing to a second temple where he is entertained with wine, food and singing women. On the second night the priests restore the refreshed god to his home. According to Mrs Abe this ritual had been performed every year for the last 1,000 years. As Japanese say this about all their festivals and as most turn out to have originated only a few decades earlier, I did not stumble through the deer park in the dark and freezing cold with high hopes.

As I climbed the hill, I could smell the deer droppings and hear the rustling of the animals themselves. Otherwise a black silence enveloped me. The path broadened to an avenue lined with stone lanterns. Here a 200-strong crowd had gathered. At the top of the avenue stood an inconspicuous temple rather like a garden shed amongst the trees. I found a place next to an elderly couple. They came to the festival every year, they said. I asked why. They looked away uncomfortably. It was hard to explain, admitted the old man finally. It was just something they did. Male and female priests wearing gold robes and stiff, black conical hats walked past followed by supplicants in fur coats. The waiting crowd gossiped and laughed with the casual, irreverent air common to Japanese festivals.

An old man hobbled up and down instructing us through a loud hailer to extinguish every sort of light including cigarettes. We waited in the dark, the crowd now silent. In front of the temple burned a fire. Two priests caught up staves of glowing wood from the flames and ran, one on each side, down the avenue, trailing parallel lines of sparks behind them to purify the ground. Out of the blackness rose a murmur. The murmur grew loud and insistent. Priests and priestesses dressed in white and carrying branches of laurel took shape in the gloom. They passed us unheeding, emitting hoarse cries, half running, half shuffling down the avenue. One group who passed more closely bunched than the rest bore the god in a palanquin shielded by thick foliage and preceded by a cloud of incense, heavy and unexpected on the night air.

Something ancient and primitive like a shadow passed over us. We turned after the priests and stumbled down the avenue, the moon shining directly in front. We took the steps pressed together, the parallel lines of fire and the smell of incense before us. No one spoke or exchanged glances. People were neither friendly nor unfriendly. Human contact had become irrelevant. The ritual in the dark had erased all sense of individuality. We plunged forward as if part of a torrent or a wind or an avalanche. Suddenly I panicked and began to struggle. Seeing a space I pushed through and clambered up the bank and on to the grass. Below me the crush tumbled silently down the hillside. I did not join them but ran alongside, tripping over rabbit holes and squelching into deer droppings. At the last moment, I had wanted something very simple: I had wanted to be myself.

At the bottom of the hill, the priests delivered the god to a wooden shrine smothered in branches. On each side two priests sat on the ground feeding wood into burning braziers. For a while there was no sound but the murmur of the crowd and the crackling of wood. Then a flute began to play. The priests emerged from a canopy where they had been refreshing themselves, formed a line and bowed to the god. Two priests slowly beat a drum the size of a man as lacquered trays of fish, cabbage, carrots and apples were passed along the line up to the god. After the food followed casks of sake. Then the priests dispersed and two women dressed in a style fashionable a thousand years before plucked at the samisen. It was now three in the morning. The ceremony had been going on for four hours. Despite the promise of more rituals, I returned to bed. In the end it was not the priests or the ancient forms of entertainment devised for the god but the slow fall down the avenue and the loss of self, eerie and oddly seductive, that lingered in the mind.

7

Mr Sato finally introduced me to the rock band. They were holding a meeting before a concert. As this was the Kobokan, the table had been laid with a clean cloth and decorated with carnations and lilies. Female volunteer workers served sushi and Coca-Cola. All five members of the rock band had grown up in the Kobokan's Children's Home in Karuizawa. They displayed a warmth and frankness rare for Japanese. I got on particularly well with Tachi, the drummer, who was small and energetic with very white skin. He announced to the art master, 'You are always starting to say things you never finish. Why don't you say what you really think.'

The band discussed what photographs to project on to the wall while they played. The art director and Mr Sato wanted images from nature. Tachi and I demanded socially relevant photographs, 'of homeless in the Bronx' said Tachi. I said why not the homeless in Oshiage, the area served by the Kobokan, or, failing that, homeless at least in the Far East, but this suggestion was ignored. The art director and Mr Sato did not want homeless wherever they came from. 'We think pine trees and flowers more atmospheric,' said Mr Sato. Tachi grinned. 'Oh all right,' he said amidst laughter, 'we've got to give way to our elders and betters.' As the meeting broke up, he said to me, 'You were on my side. We shared the same ideas but they turned out to be wrong. I tried to say 'not wrong, just different' but this was impossible. The Japanese language does not distinguish between these two terms;

chigau means both different and wrong. Tachi spoke warmly of the Children's Home and its director, Miss Fujino. 'When you need someone on your side, she's there. She never lets you down.' For a moment he looked sad then he cheered up and urged me to go on a visit.

Shortly afterwards Mr Sato invited my family to spend the weekend at the Children's Home in Karuizawa. On the drive down he admitted to my husband that he often joined the rock band as the lead singer. For the three and a half hour drive we discussed rock music. Mr Sato was impressed to hear that I had attended pop concerts in Hyde Park and even, at the age of fifteen, seen Joe Cocker play. 'You must lecture our young men on your experiences,' he said earnestly as if we were discussing a war.

The road climbed through misshapen mountains to a plateau covered in forest. Since the 1870s foreigners had come to Karuizawa to escape the heat of a Tokyo summer. It soon became the fashionable spot for rich Tokyoites to own summer houses. In amongst these and deep in a forest stood the Children's Home. A mountain rose abruptly behind. I had warned my husband to expect the minimum in the way of comfort and food. Instead we were shown into a pretty, warm tatami room and served a delicious dinner during which the Home's director, Miss Fujino, came in with a present for Gabriella. Miss Fujino was in her sixties. Tiny, exquisitely dressed in dark blue, her grey hair cut into a bob, she resembled one of my daughter's Japanese dolls except for her mouth which was wide and curling. Gabriella stared as if expecting at any moment for her to be picked up and packed away in a toy box. Miss Fujino had started working in the Children's Home in 1947. Her aunt was a friend of the first Japanese director, also a woman. 'I was very idealistic,' said Miss Fujino, all the time watching her staff to see that they served the food correctly. It was she, I realized, who was responsible for the comfort and charm of the Home.

After the war a number of Tokyo's orphans began to congregate around Ueno station. Some were collected up and dispatched to the Children's Home. Miss Fujino explained in her low voice, 'Before the war this was a camp site only used in summer time. When the children arrived, there was nothing. It was also very cold. Many of the children got frost bite. If they caught a cold they woke up to find their snot frozen. We begged potatoes and pumpkins from the local farmers. The children collected logs from the hillside so we could boil the water for rice.' All this the staff paid for themselves. They received nothing from the government until 1948 when under the orders of the American Occupation, the Japanese government passed the Child Welfare Act. The site was recognized as an official Children's Home receiving children from the Tokyo metropolitan area. 'We decided to stay small. We have thirty children and fifteen staff.'

The Home has always concentrated on emotionally damaged children. 'We take children who have been beaten, had their nails pulled off or have been burnt with lighted cigarettes. Most of these children are from white-collar rather than blue-collar families. Money is not the problem.' My husband and I looked at each other astonished. We had never read or heard anything about child abuse in Japan. Japanese newspapers reported cases from the States or Britain. They treated abuse as a purely Western phenomenon to such an extent that we had come to believe so too.

At this point a boy of about eleven entered excitedly. He ran up to Miss Fujino who put her arms around him. 'What happened?' she asked, stroking his cheek. He belonged to a choir which had just given a public performance. He was one of the soloists. 'I've brought you a present,' said Miss Fujino pointing to a parcel. He rushed over, pulled off the wrapping and held up a briefcase. He exclaimed with pleasure, tucked it under his arm and walked delightedly around the room. After he had gone, Miss Fujino explained that his mother was the wife of one of Japan's leading gangsters who had got pregnant while her husband was in prison. After the birth, she left the baby with the authorities, promising to return. Miss Fujino, who had little time for the parents of her children, said severely, 'Of course she hasn't. He knows she never will but still, even now, he dreams that one day she will reclaim him.'

The next day Mr Sato showed us the Home, a series of log cabins around a camp site surrounded with trees. Each cabin held about five children and a member of staff who acted as a parent. The boys played ball with Gabriella, demonstrated how to whistle through bits of grass or urged my husband to pick them up and throw them around 'roughly please'. Gabriella watched intently. She was very keen on Peter Pan and I had explained that these were some of the Lost Boys. 'Will they fly after tea?' she asked.

In the television room I found the children crowded around an exhausted Miss Fujino. Two adolescent girls massaged her neck and shoulders. A large fat boy patted her hand. 'She's not well,' they said desperately to me. Miss Fujino shook her head and smiled. She had, I was later told, just been diagnosed with Parkinson's Disease.

We drank tea from a china pot decorated with rose buds. Miss Fujino believed in the efficacy of pretty things. She applied the same principle to the children in her care. When they arrived she let them do what they wanted. 'At first they are tense and silent. Then they become very demanding and selfish, but that's the start of a relationship with a damaged child. I greet that first bout of bad behaviour as a good friend. If they ask me for toys, I buy them. If they want money, I give it to them. After two or three weeks of this, they will return from school one day, announce that they are hungry and open the fridge door. When they do that you know they have relaxed. Unconsciously they have become one of the family.'

Miss Fujino's assistant came into the room. I recognized him as the curly-haired man who had failed to learn his lines for the Kobokan's Nativity play. He picked up the china cup and looked at it with bemusement. Tomo had come to the Children's Home as a baby and had been taken special care of by Miss Fujino. 'She had very strange ways,' he said with a shout of laughter. Once the head of the local school had summoned her. He had decided to suspend Tomo for bad behaviour. Tomo said, 'So do you know what she did? Mr Sato had come to visit so she gave us money and sent us off to a shrine festival. It was my first holiday ever. Another time, when the head had threatened expulsion, she took me to a really posh establishment for dinner. "You've got to learn how to behave in public," she said. That was how she punished me!'

I asked if she did not have trouble from the local schools. Surely they found her attitude incomprehensible? She agreed that they urged her to punish the children while 'I'm always begging them not to'. What about when they left the children's home, I persisted, how did these children brought up in a Christian tradition fit into Japanese society? At this she looked sad and said that other Homes put emphasis on outward show rather than the person within. 'They want to turn out good citizens. I cannot change the manner of my children but at least I can equip them with a warm heart. I have to admit they don't fit easily into Japanese society. When they join a company, the other employees dismiss them as uncouth. I can only hope that someone will spot their generous nature and take them up.' She encouraged her children to be brave and persevere. Often they came to see her to talk over the difference between the Kobokan and Japanese society. 'The real thing is in the Kobokan,' they insisted.

I asked about the success of her methods. 'With enough love, children do recover,' she insisted. Many had settled down, visiting the Children's Home with husbands, wives and children for the traditional holidays spent by Japanese with their families. Others were more of a problem. She pointed to her assistant and shook her head. Tomo had gone to Tokyo when he was twenty and lost money on the horses. Unable to pay his debts, he ran away, travelling around the country doing odd jobs and sending money back. He never let anyone know where he was. It took three years to discharge the debt. He reappeared and entered university to study social work. 'Punch perm here,' said Mr Sato referring to Tomo's thick, curly hair, 'graduated finally at thirty-four. Almost a grandfather, we said.' He returned to the Children's Home to work. 'Some take longer than others to come right,' said Miss Fujino with her slow smile.

When I told Mrs Abe about our trip to Karuizawa she looked puzzled. 'There are no abused children in Japan,' she said. 'We

141

read about such wicked things but of course they only take place in the West.'

'They have cars like that in America, don't they?' said an astonished Mrs Yamada. Dressed in kimono and looking lovely she was coming out to lunch with me to celebrate my fourth New Year in Japan. I had offered to drive. Our car was dented and scratched from years of manoeuvring around Tokyo's alleyways. We had long ceased to bother having it repaired. Mrs Yamada eyed the trailing bumper, half held up with tape, and climbed in.

We had lunch in the Arabic Café, which despite its name and the photographs on the walls of languid, adolescent sultans, served French food. Mrs Yamada admitted that her husband's health had improved. She still spent four or five hours a day in the hospital. She said in the cheery way Japanese employ to hide their true feelings, 'How quickly the time passes there. So much to do. When I get home, I am too sleepy to work!' Misled by her tone I asked if she planned a reconciliation. She paused, looking down, the tip of her tongue pushed out between her lips. Finally she said, 'Perhaps it is very oriental of me but it is not a question of forgiveness. That implies I am on a higher level than my husband and I am certainly not that. No, it is a question of failing to understand him. I was actually thinking of returning to my parents.'

She explained that she was an only child. 'Mine is not a famous family but it has been around for a long time, nineteen generations to be exact.' She wanted to resume her maiden name. She thought she was being unusually frank with me; instead she had increased my confusion. She had no children, I said as gently as I could, what was the point of taking back her maiden name? 'Mine will be the last name on the family tombstone. I must close the curtain on our family history.'

Over coffee she said that her husband could not talk, 'but I think he is waving the white flag'. I pressed her again about a reconciliation. Mrs Yamada obviously had not expected me, a Westerner, to caution against divorce. This time she burst out, 'If I forgive him I will have to be responsible for this other woman's child for the rest of my life.' She folded her hands together and we did not raise the matter again. On both sides, it was an unsatisfactory and puzzling conversation.

As we drove back, a man on a scooter stopped us. He wore white gloves and carried a clipboard. He stared at the immaculate Mrs Yamada. 'A lady like you should be careful about driving around in a car like this. It could be very dangerous,' he said severely before bending down to hitch the bumper back into place. It fell off in his hands. Frantically he tried to stick back the worn tape. The bumper fell off again. I got out of the car, took the bumper from him and put it in the boot. Then I drove off. Mrs Yamada, forgetting her troubles, forgetting even the stiff *obi* forcing her to sit upright, relaxed back into her seat and started to laugh.

My English lessons at the Kobokan had met with unexpected success. Before lunch I stood up and talked about some aspect of England which had become distilled in my mind by several years absence into a pleasurable caricature of itself. One week I described a friend's evening out with her husband to celebrate her birthday. The old people were amazed to hear individuals enjoyed birthdays. They had never celebrated one of their own until they started lunching at the Kobokan. Once a month Mrs Goto bought or made cards for everyone born during that period in which friends and volunteer workers wrote affectionate messages. At the end of a special lunch complete with English tea and homemade biscuits one elderly guest would stand up, bow, say a few words and present the card. Afterwards we burst into 'Happy Birthday Dear Honourable Everyone'.

I described an evening out in the West. The old ladies looked astonished. Their husbands had never taken them anywhere. I explained how the husband held open the door of the restaurant for his wife. For a moment there was silence then everyone burst out laughing. 'Never ever in Japan,' said Mrs Komita wiping her eyes. The husband, I continued, helped his wife take off her coat

143

before the *maitre d'* led them to the table, the wife proceeding first and waiting while the husband offered her a chair. This caused so much amazement that Mrs Goto and I were called upon to mime the proceedings three times over. The men shook their heads. The women glanced at me wistfully. 'But has this really happened to you?' they asked.

Afterwards I stood in the hall waving goodbye for no one departs anywhere in Japan without a leaving committee. Finally I bent down to put on my own shoes. Mrs Komita had been looking at me hard. Suddenly she darted forward and patted my stomach. 'Pregnant are we?' she said. I nodded, confused. I had not even told my husband.

The next week Mrs Goto asked if she could announce publicly 'the happy event' as she put it. Was that the custom, I asked, trying to stall her. 'Yes,' she replied firmly. I had to stand up in front of the forty old people while Mrs Goto declared that I had 'cause for celebration'. Everyone made a great fuss. Mr Sato blushed. 'Are you sure you can come next week?' he asked anxiously as if at any moment I might fall into pieces on the floor. Mrs Komita hugged me continuously then presented me with a tiny china ball painted with roses which tinkled when I shook it. 'Hang it on your purse for luck,' she begged.

After lunch the old people planned their annual trip to Karuizawa to stay in the Kobokan's Children's Home. The trip included a visit to a temple and an *onsen*. I would be seven months gone by then. I announced my determination to join the party. 'But do you know Japanese *onsen*?' they queried. 'I love hot springs,' I said, 'but you will have to excuse my strange shape.' Two old men hesitated as they registered the image of a large, pregnant, foreign woman stepping naked into an *onsen*, then broke into giggles. 'It is not mixed!' they hastily assured me. One patted my hand. I was not to worry, he said. They were all grandparents and so would be able to take care of me and give me good advice on the trip.

At first being pregnant in Japan offered compensations. No one

144

expected me to look good enough to pose for a magazine cover or do a deal from a hospital bed. Japanese still view pregnancy as a mystical state in which to luxuriate. A gangster, passing me in the street near the Kobokan, started back, awestruck, his eyes riveted to my bulge. He exclaimed, 'I've never seen anything like it! What have you got in there, three boys and a cat?' Then he leaned forward and reverently rubbed my stomach.

Pregnancy had the same effect on the Japanese police. I had attended a parents' meeting at my daughter's Japanese nursery school. Twenty mothers and I sat in a circle on child-sized chairs in our children's classroom. About half the mothers were working-class, the other half professional women in suits. One by one each woman voiced her anxieties concerning her child, prefaced by a catalogue, seemingly obligatory, of their failings as a mother. Potty training caused one woman so much worry that she had gone to her local temple for advice. The teachers made soothing noises. Gabriella, they said to me, was happy except that she refused to pee in front of anyone at potty time. This drew an admiring, 'She's a real little lady!' After mutual bowing, we left to find the police had towed away our cars.

Twenty minutes later they were regretting their officiousness. A spring snow storm left the station full of drenched mothers and screaming, wet children. We lined up in front of an old man in a hand-knitted, cream waistcoat, his cuffs encased in black plastic covers. Two young girls in uniform hovered next to him. 'Do you admit to your fault,' he asked me. I said I was a stupid foreigner who had parked in the same spot as the other Japanese mothers. This, as I intended, caused great embarrassment. It is a Japanese duty to set a good example to foreigners. I paused then bowed and apologized. Everyone looked relieved. Here was a foreigner who knew how to behave. They then discovered I did not know my registration number or even the make of the car. 'It's dirty grey,' I said hopefully. As a number of cars had been towed away from the same spot, they took a long time to assign me the wrong car.

An hour and a half passed. The other mothers had all left. Exhaustion suddenly seized me. I said I was pregnant and not feeling well. Immediately they expressed consternation. Was I too hot or too cold? What could they do? Papers were now picked up, put down and shuffled with increased vigour. The girls produced an impressive form and pointed to where I had to sign my name. They then placed in front of me a pot of black ink and shreds of white tissue. They wanted to fingerprint me. Finger-printing is an emotive issue in Japan. All foreigners are fingerprinted, even Koreans who have lived in the country for two or three generations. I decided to take a stand. I drew myself up. I had received a Japanese lesson that morning on criminal types which I now recalled with enthusiasm. I said in Japanese, 'I noticed that you asked none of the Japanese mothers for their fingerprints so why are you asking me? In England only criminals are finger-printed. I am neither a murderer, an armed robber, a pickpocket or a thief so I refuse to comply.' The girl appeared in a state of shock. 'It's all right, don't worry, don't worry,' assured her companion hastily putting away the ink.

I did not have enough money to pay the fine so the next morning found me once again at the police station. All the policemen asked after my health, patting their stomachs to indicate the baby. The old man, this time in a black knitted waistcoat, showed me to the door, holding it open until I had passed through. 'Please take good care of yourself,' he called after me. It was a sentiment not shared by other segments of Japanese society towards pregnant women, but that I was only to discover later.

146

8

Mrs Abe also stopped me in the street but she was not interested in my pregnancy. Instead she gripped my arm. 'Have you heard the latest news on the cherry blossom?' she asked. From March one question preoccupies the Japanese. When will the cherry trees flower in their area? The first blossoms are seen in Kyushu, Japan's most southern island, and thereafter the front moves north. The blooms are a pale, fragile pink and last less than a week. Companies take the day off, retire to the parks and hold noisy parties beneath the blooms. 'Only in Japan does the whole country come to a halt so people can go and look at flowers,' was how Charlie put it.

Mrs Abe and I had already had one argument on the subject. Mrs Abe described Japanese cherry blossom with an almost spiritual enthusiasm. Western cherry blossom she dismissed as vulgar. 'Like neon lights and it lasts so long which spoils everything!' Cherry blossom season was a time to reflect on the beauty and transience of life, she added. She herself would be at a well-known beauty spot outside Tokyo doing just that. She was wearing a fetching dress in light colours. Would her father-in-law be joining her, I asked. 'His falcon is moulting and he does not like to leave her,' she said, tweaking aside a dead leaf from one of my pot plants.

At Mrs Abe's prodding, I took my daughter for a picnic in Aoyama cemetery. It sits on a hill in the middle of Tokyo, a split of greenery with the city lapping up on every side. Two avenues

147

of cherry trees bisect the graveyard. In spring their gnarled branches transform into tunnels of pale pink blossom luminous and enclosing like the whorls of a shell. I sat and gazed at the blossom while my daughter played amongst the graves. These were stone pillars about four feet tall surrounded by a low balustrade, a gate and steps, and made, as Gabriella discovered, perfect play houses. As she prepared cherry blossom soup for me, family groups passed carrying baskets of flowers and sticks of incense for the dead. The women arranged the flowers then removed small brooms concealed behind the tombstones to sweep the grave.

The first sign of the cherry blossom festival proved to be workers in coolie hats, their arms full of beer cans, plastic mats and paper bags discarded from the previous night's celebrations. It was now six in the evening. Junior office workers, sent early to claim a spot, spread mats big enough for twenty or thirty people beneath the trees. Girls in the company uniform arranged cans of beer and packets of rice crackers in the centre of the mats. They then took off their shoes, placed them neatly along the edge of the mat, and knelt with a charming and respectful attitude to await the arrival of their male colleagues. I overheard one say to her friend, 'I would much rather spend the evening with my boyfriend. The boss and the others will just get drunk and expect us to laugh at their stupid jokes.'

Some parties had already begun the business of drinking, the participants occasionally pausing to raise a hand to the falling blossom. Behind the graves enterprising revellers had to set up gas cylinders and even generators. A few groups had food sizzling on hot plates. As dusk turned to night they lit paper lanterns strung overhead. Karaoke video sets for those presumably bored by cherry blossom and moonlight flashed views of Hong Kong and Hawaii. A drunken middle-aged man seized a microphone and launched into My Way.

Oblivious of the noise, two old men sat straight-backed on a tatami mat. Each wrote with a calligraphy brush. They were composing haiku, they explained. They had come here every year since the war. It was traditional at cherry blossom time. You sat with a friend beneath the trees and competed to see who could write the most poignant lines of poetry. They offered me sake and Gabriella a rice cracker.

On the way down the hill we passed crowds of men and women carrying beer up the avenue. Groups of anxious office workers waited at the side to welcome senior staff and point out the company spot. Above them the blossom shone against the darkening sky with its own eerie effulgence.

When I mentioned the karaoke machines to Mrs Abe she said 'Oh'. It was her habit when presented with an unpalatable fact about Japan. It meant that she did not believe in its existence. Sometimes she drew the 'Oh' out longer. This indicated that she accepted the existence of the karaoke machine, but blamed it on me, the contaminating foreigner. If I had not seen the karaoke machine, it would not have been there.

A few days later the Kobokan telephoned me. The optimum day for cherry blossom viewing had arrived in Sumida-ku. Mrs Goto reported that the blossom was at its fullest and, after days of rain, the sky finally clear. All thirty-five old people and half a dozen volunteers were off to picnic. I was dispatched to the stone-floored kitchen where staff in white gumboots and head scarves prepared the food. Despite its poverty, the Kobokan owned a number of fine *bento* or black lacquer boxes in which Japanese traditionally serve lunch. Each person received a box divided into compartments in order to hold a variety of foods. 'You have to make it look as appetising as possible,' explained Mrs Komita as we arranged fried chicken next to rice cooked with slithers of bamboo on beds of lettuce then sprinkled the whole with tiny chopped leaves.

The Kobokan also boasted two mini-buses in which we now packed the forty-odd boxes followed by plastic sheets, cushions, glasses, sake, thermos flasks of tea, chopsticks, ash trays and a ghetto blaster whose function only became clear later on. We drove to Sumida river lined on both sides by cherry trees. Behind the thin smear of pink, factories belched smoke and express ways

149

shook with lorries. 'Isn't it beautiful?' said Mrs Komita digging me in the side with her elbow.

The volunteer workers, all young and good-looking men (it seemed the qualification for the Kobokan), found a hollow where we could sit enclosed by cherry trees. We laid out the mats, took off our shoes and sat down, the shoes arranged neatly around the edge. As we ate, the men toasted themselves in sake while the women sipped tea. I found myself next to Toki Kinzo, a tiny old man with sparkling eyes beneath eyebrows set high and wide apart. In my honour he burst into Rule Britannia, which he had learnt at school some seventy years before when a member of the British Royal family visited Japan. He confided that in the old days cherry blossom viewing had proved a far more raucous affair with everybody getting drunk and carrying on. 'Now we are all old and serious,' he added with a wink.

Mr Toki was in his eighties. His family had moved to Tokyo from the countryside when he was three. He was typical of the neighbourhood and his class. The lives of old people like Mr Toki never ceased to amaze me. They took for granted the extraordi- nary deprivations they had suffered. Their small stature and the collapsed spines of many of the women provided a constant reminder of a hungry childhood. Their spartan attitudes contrasted with the appearance and demeanour of their grandchildren, large, slovenly creatures who slouched in their seats, lived off ham- burgers and threw away almost new clothes, electrical goods and furniture. Old people like Mr Toki who still wore kimono and walked the streets in his underwear in the heat of summer typified Japan's past far better than Mrs Abe for all her pretensions as a guardian of Japanese tradition. Modern Japanese showed no interest in these last remnants of pre-war Japan. The old people represented an embarrassing period, failure in the Second World War and the first invasion of the country by a foreign power. Unable to mythologize this particular past, Japanese simply ignored it. Various old people complained, 'Our grandchildren never ask us about the past. They act as if it did not happen.'

When I suggested to Mr Sato that he record the old people's stories he looked vague. 'Would anyone be interested?' he asked.

In the 1920s Tokyoites considered Oshiage, the area surrounding the Kobokan, lovely enough for a day trip. It boasted streams, ponds and a river clean enough to fish in. Only one factory stood in the area then. People raised chickens, bred goldfish in the former rice paddies or kept pack horses to carry baggage into the city. Mr Toki's parents sold goldfish feed which they delivered in wheelbarrows. They put their children to work at an early age. Too puny to push the barrow, the eight-year-old Mr Toki carried sacks of feed on his back instead. 'They were so heavy you can't imagine,' he said, shaking his head at the memory. Then he brightened. 'But I've got a healthy lower back and strong legs as a result.' He stretched out a leg for me to admire. 'My contemporaries are always complaining of back problems but not me!'

In those days poor people never owned a new home he explained. They waited until a rich person pulled down his house in the centre of Tokyo. From the left-overs the poor constructed their dwellings. Mr Toki lived in a row of wooden houses crammed close together. Behind stretched fields where children played. His house measured about nine yards by seven. 'That must have been a bit of a squash,' I said when he told me he had three sisters. 'There wasn't just us. We shared the house with a family of six,' he said, amazed that I should think the Toki family had an entire house to themselves. They could not afford heating during Tokyo's bitter winters. Occasionally the children dressed in something thicker, a padded jacket perhaps, 'but no one liked to waste money on clothes,' he explained. Whatever the weather, his parents constantly sent him and his sisters to play outside, not surprising considering the lack of space. 'We were called Children of the Wind,' recalled Mr Toki.

Mr Toki remembered watching the building of the Kobokan on a piece of swampy ground near his home. The Canadian missionaries had named 1 September 1923 as the opening day. It was round about lunchtime went on Mr Toki. A typhoon had just passed out to sea leaving behind a strong wind and drizzle. Children were returning home for lunch after the school ceremony to mark the start of a new term. The eleven-year-old Mr Toki, who only went to school when there was nothing else for him to do, had just delivered a sack of goldfish feed to a customer near the Kobokan. He paused to admire the first Western building to rise out of that slum neighbourhood. The boy had never beheld anything so magnificent or so exotic. The missionaries, unlike their parishioners, could afford new materials. The gleaming red roof looked like something out of a dream. Exhausted after carrying the feed, he sank down to rest under the eaves of a house.

It was at that moment that the Great Kanto earthquake struck Tokyo. It measured 7.9 on the Richter scale. Over 700 aftershocks followed in the next three days. The cooking fires lit to prepare lunch spread quickly, the flames consuming about a third of the city's homes, mostly in the poorer areas along the Sumida river. A hundred thousand people died, the majority in the conflagration that followed the quake.

Stones rolling like cannon balls off the roof above him alerted Toki to the disaster. The houses opposite lurched from side to side. The boy clung to the ground that trembled and buckled beneath him. The quake passed and he scrambled up only to be hurled into the gutter by an aftershock. A man with a child under his arm dashed out of a house just as it collapsed. Toki lay in the gutter gasping and shaking. He knew he should go home but he could not move. All around people were recovering from their shock and beginning to scream. Then, above the screams, he heard a roar which grew louder and louder. A woman ran past him. 'The tidal wave is coming, the wave is coming,' she yelled. 'I was seriously afraid,' admitted Mr Toki. He lay in the gutter and prepared to die. Time passed and the roaring ceased. When Toki found himself still alive, he got up and went home.

He found his family unharmed and their house still standing. His parents, anxious about less fortunate neighbours, gave their son one yen to go and buy food for the homeless in the street. This was a fabulous amount, equal to about fifty pounds now, and more money than the young Toki knew existed. He pocketed the coin reverently and set off to walk out of the city the length of 'three stations on a railway line', as he put it, to the store. His parents had told him to select whatever he wanted. On a boy used to deprivation this made a deep impression. So much so that whenever Mr Toki recalled the earthquake, 'I remember the fear I felt much less than the vast and unexpected happiness of having so much money to spend on whatever food I liked.'

Mrs Goto now passed around cherry blossom cake made of bean curd and wrapped in cherry leaves. We ate it with a slither of bamboo. The evening of the earthquake Toki and his family watched flames over 100 metres high consume Tokyo. On the second day the fires died down and his parents sent him on another mission. The nature of their work meant they had plenty of rice in the house. Toki's mother worried that her sister and a number of her husband's relatives who lived on the other side of Tokyo might be hungry. She instructed her son to cross the city with supplies. They tied the sack of rice on his back with the cloth used by women to carry their children. Looters, they hoped, would mistake the precious food for a baby.

The eleven-year-old boy set off across the devastated city. The earthquake had destroyed all the bridges along the Sumida river. Toki picked his way precariously over the wreckage. On the other side he turned south and followed the river bank. Terrible sights greeted him. Charred corpses lay three or four deep where people had rushed to the water only to be caught by giant balls of fire bowling down the river. Toki left the Sumida with relief and turned West towards the Ginza. He navigated by its red-brick, Western-style buildings which had survived the fire. On every side stretched the charred remains of traditional wooden houses.

Amongst the devastation the boy saw boards scribbled with messages planted in the rubble of former homes. 'They announced who had survived and where they could be found,' he remembered. At Ueno station he stopped to eat the rice balls his mother had provided for the journey. Messages painted on scraps of wood covered the station statue. He found them unbearably poignant. Seventy years later he could still remember one which read, 'Will any member of the Masuda family please wait here for Hisoko and baby'. He explained, 'I have never forgotten her childish writing. I imagined her not much older than me and all alone except for the infant.' It took him six hours to reach his aunt's house.

The picnic now over, one old lady in her eighties suddenly burst into song. Miss Otoi's face still displayed the vestiges of great beauty despite age, cropped hair and baggy trousers. Until this moment she had never joined in anything, preferring to sit sullenly in a corner. Her sudden enthusiasm inspired her neighbour to unzip what I had taken for a knitting bag and produce a samisen. A volunteer picked up the ghetto blaster and hurried to their side, holding out the microphone. Against the twanging of the samisen, Miss Otoi warbled a plaintive Japanese folk song. I had listened to these before without much interest but Miss Otoi infused her singing with a strength and passion that transfixed me. Disregarding the microphone and, for that matter, her audience, she raised a smiling face to the blossom and sang with all her heart. When she finished everyone broke into applause. The volunteer passed the microphone to other old men and women who launched into song. The music rose about us as petals of blossom slowly settled on the heads of the elderly.

'Dancing time,' announced Mrs Komita, scarcely able to contain herself. This was her speciality. We packed away the picnic and strolled down to the water's edge. Under Mrs Komita's leadership we formed a circle. The steps from Japanese folk dances reflect peasant preoccupations, hoeing the ground, harvesting rice or digging for coal. The simple movements of work are followed by a graceful fluttering of hands at the sky, the whole repeated endlessly. Miss Otoi continued to sing to the strumming of her neighbour's samisen. We danced as Japanese have done for hundreds of years to music without, for Western ears, tune or rhythm. The dance exerted a hypnotic effect. It required not individual grace but the submission of the chorus line. I concentrated on the old lady in front of me, on turning and waving exactly as she did. When I succeeded, a great pleasure overtook me. I forgot myself, felt only the movements and saw only the circle. Then Mrs Komita paused and the spell broke. I noticed that a crowd had gathered to watch the spectacle of a large, pregnant foreigner who thought she had become a small, elderly Japanese. On the river two *yakuza* in dark glasses and a red speedboat, appropriately named Miami Promise, caught sight of me and whirled about in a spray of water to hover, staring incredulously. I sat down on a bench and said I would watch the next number.

Tramps whom we had displaced gathered in a nearby gazebo to gaze resentfully at our enjoyment. One, dressed in black with longish hair, looked like an intellectual. I imagined him, after years of study and sacrifice, failing the final exam and from there toppling downwards to his present condition. He had left his belongings next to me on the bench, a small black suitcase and a bar of Camay soap.

On the way back to the bus I asked Mrs Komita about Miss Otoi's accomplishments. 'She must have been beautiful and she sings so well. Was she geisha?' Mrs Komita, normally frank, appeared uneasy. Finally she said, 'Not geisha exactly. She was part of the *mizu shobai*, the entertainment business.'

The cherry blossom party continued to have a rejuvenating effect on Miss Otoi. The next week she arrived with a clutch of photographs. One revealed Miss Otoi in her early twenties, arrestingly lovely in winter kimono. Her expression held me. She appeared lost and dumbfounded as if shaken by a series of nasty shocks. Within the beautifully composed folds of her kimono, her fingers lay bent with tension, the knuckles rigid. I asked if she had been married by then. Miss Otoi shook her head angrily. She said that circumstances had prevented any man marrying her. 'I live alone. I have no husband or child.' Miss Otoi then remarked that she had heard I had written a book about 1930s Shanghai. She had an aunt there whom she had never visited. She had gone to Manchuria instead, at the age of seventeen. This photograph had been taken on her return to Tokyo.

I stared again at the photograph. Groping for words I asked Miss

Otoi if she had ever sung for the Japanese troops. Miss Otoi's face darkened. 'Never!' she exclaimed bitterly, 'I never sang for them.' The explanation for Mrs Komita's careful description came to me. Miss Otoi had been a 'comfort woman'. When the Japanese army invaded Manchuria, its commanders feared their troops' propensity to rape might worsen resistance amongst the local population so they set up military brothels or 'comfort' stations. The Japanese government always insisted these brothels were private establishments. Documents discovered recently in the Defence Agency library in Tokyo prove that the government and the army set up the brothels and kidnapped and imprisoned thousands of women, many of whom died servicing forty or fifty men a day. Mostly the girls came from China, Korea and the Philippines. Some Japanese girls already in the entertainment business had been lured to China and sold. I imagined Miss Otoi, trained as a geisha, tricked by a pimp into the hell of an army brothel in Manchuria. How had she escaped? I guessed her beauty had caught the fancy of someone important and he had brought her back to Tokyo. She stared at me, her eyes suddenly canny, then shook her head. 'Of course there is a lot I could say but no one speaks of the war now. I don't want to ruin any reputations. The men concerned are all old and we should show old men respect, shouldn't we?' She grimaced.

During lunch Miss Otoi broke into a sudden song and looked to her neighbours for a corresponding enthusiasm. Their attention was elsewhere. Her singing seemed to be everything to her, to make up for all she lacked. When she sang she appeared warm, kindly and fun-loving. Then she stopped and her face resumed its closed expression.

Afterwards a few of us withdrew into a small room to drink tea and coffee. We called this the *kissaten*, a Japanese word for coffee shop. Over a gas stove Mrs Goto prepared coffee which she offered with cinnamon sticks and *omocha*, frothy, bitter green tea served in earthenware bowls. This treat cost the old people two

156

hundred yen. Mrs Komita always came and was responsible for the rowdy atmosphere, mostly at the expense of her husband.

One old lady described a visit to the Komita's during which Mrs Komita answered the telephone. 'Oh you should have heard the voice she put on, all sugary sweet, then she put her hand over the mouthpiece and bellowed at her husband like this,' and she spat out some words. 'Well what good is he?' protested Mrs Komita amidst the laughter. 'He's retired now and spends four hours every day in the *pachinko* parlour. He's nothing but trouble. Even when he's at home he never says a word. Not one! I chat to the rice cooker. We have very interesting conversations my rice cooker and me.' Another old lady broke in. 'Maybe if you kept quiet for a moment, he'd have a chance to speak,' she advised. Mrs Komita snorted. 'What's he got to talk about anyway? Japanese men have nothing to say for themselves,' she added turning to me. Her friend nodded. 'We wives dread it when they retire and are at home all day. It's our generation who are getting divorced. We can't stand having this stranger around, unable to string two words together except to give orders.' 'Do this, do that,' added another old lady in agreement. The one old man bold enough to join the group nodded and smiled throughout the exchange. It was as if they were discussing a typhoon, regrettable of course, but that was what typhoons did.

The usual boxes, biscuit tins and balls of string which Japanese consider necessary for life packed the room. On the wall hung a picture of an English hunt. I tried to explain this to my amazed elderly neighbour. Finally, she held up her hands and shook her head. It was all, she indicated, beyond her. The conversation had moved on to Mrs Komita's son who at thirty-six still lived with his parents. 'He doesn't dare marry,' chuckled one old lady. Mrs Komita described the rules she forced him to follow. 'She pretends to despise him but really she's delighted to have him at home,' whispered my neighbour. The old lady on the other side leaned across me. 'Of course she is. He gives her all his salary!'

Throughout this exchange Miss Otoi sat silently looking out of the window at a piece of waste ground. Bundles of straw suddenly began to hurtle down from the upper storeys of the Kobokan. A few minutes later three boys of nine or ten appeared and started to gather up the straw, pausing to throw it up into the air or down one another's shirts. With great difficulty Miss Otoi, her eyes not leaving the boys, heaved herself up. Painfully she made her way to the window and stood there, leaning on her stick, drinking in the scene below. Everybody else carried on chatting. Then she left. The next week she failed to appear. When I asked where she was, Mrs Komita shook her head. 'She went funny after the cherry blossom party, you know. She began to say strange things. Then she got a bit weak and couldn't look after herself so it was thought best to put her in an old people's home. So that's where she is, two hours from Tokyo at least, I would say.'

When I returned from the Kobokan I found Nida on the telephone to the Philippines. It proved a long and passionate call. Afterwards she banged pots into cupboards exclaiming, 'Those men, those stupid men.' Her sister had worked abroad for sixteen years in order to pay for her daughter's education. The girl had succeeded in entering a good but expensive computer training college. In her first year, at the age of eighteen, she became pregnant. Her father only discovered when she ran away for two days. The husbands of Nida, her sister and sister-in-law were shamefaced before the fury of their absent wives. Later on I found the sister in Nida's room. She said, 'She was such a good girl. We didn't think she knew about boys let alone had a boy friend.' Nida said, 'The Philippines is a Catholic country,' as if this was cause for embarrassment. I thought how Catholicism had turned a youthful escapade into the end of a life. Nida went on, 'We are shouting at our husbands, "Why didn't you watch her?"' 'They are too busy with their own girlfriends,' said her sister bitterly. Nida went on, 'They said they did but she met the boy in the afternoons and came back home for supper.' The sister got up and walked out heavily. 'She'll never get over it,' said Nida after she had seen her off. 'And she'll divorce her husband.' She looked around her room. 'What is the point if this is what our children do?' Then she went to prepare my daughter's tea.

Unimpressed by my stories of the Kobokan, Mrs Abe arranged for me to stay with a Buddhist priest and his family in a temple. She wanted me to meet an 'old fashioned family'. Like many Japanese she believed old Japan with its Confucian values of austerity, obedience and restraint to be in every way superior to its modern counterpart. Temple life, she assured me, epitomized these virtues. She found me one in a castle town in a remote part of the country. I prepared to step back into Japan's past and finally discover what really went on within the traditional Japanese family.

The temple dominated a neighbourhood of twisting lanes lined with Japanese houses. Large, old and made of wood, it had, like Buddhist temples all over Asia, a copper tiled roof that curled up at each corner. In the courtyard hung a gigantic bronze bell. To the left stood the priest's house. A dog on a chain barked at me as I pushed open the shoji screen and shouted a greeting. Nobody answered. On one side of the hall a series of tatami matted rooms, stretching the length of a tennis court, joined the house to the temple. The other side looked out over a Japanese garden. Finally the priest's wife came out of the kitchen to welcome me. She was in tears. It hardly seemed an auspicious beginning.

That night over dinner I met the priest. Despite the vastness of the house we ate in the kitchen, a small, stuffy room without a view. Takashi Yamamoto or the Revd Yamamoto as the English translation on the back of his name card proclaimed him, produced a bottle of sake in which floated gold flakes. 'Very good for the health,' he enthused and offered me a cup. His brother-in-law, a large man with a crew cut and also a priest, questioned me on my domestic arrangements. Was it true that I employed a maid? 'High-class life!' he said admiringly. Mrs Yamamoto gave me a wistful look. She had spent the meal serving us. Now she was washing up. I was treated as an honorary man. The brother-in-law continued. In my absence did the maid act as a second wife and was I on the look out for other husbands? Mrs Yamamoto hastily poured us more sake. The brother-in-law then asked my age. This produced further incredulity. Why had I waited so long to have children? Thinking it time to make some personal remarks of my own, I asked him the same question. The brother-in-law looked shamefaced. He admitted to having been a bit of a playboy. When he eventually did marry, he and his wife produced but one daughter. 'We have tried and tried but its just not much fun with an old wife,' he said. I wondered if this was the Japan Mrs Abe had envisaged me experiencing.

The Reverend explained that the temple had been founded four hundred years before by his ancestor and passed down from father to son ever since. 'I am number seventeen in line,' he added. In Japan, temples are inherited and run like a family business. The brother-in-law, seeing my astonishment, murmured that he represented the twenty-fourth generation of his temple. No such thing as a calling existed. Neither of the men expected to perform good works. They did not even know what I meant by the expression. The temple was a lucrative concern. Every prayer and blessing had its price carefully recorded by Mrs Yamamoto in the accounts book. Baffled by a religious institution which eschewed charity and priests who were playboys, I went to bed. Outside I glimpsed my lacy underwear hanging up to dry between the white *tabi* (split-toed socks) and kimono of the priests.

In the morning I searched for the bathroom. Rooms appeared in no particular order and with no apparent purpose. Despite its vastness the house had the same transitory atmosphere that permeates all Japanese homes. It was as if the occupants had just moved in or were just about to leave. Incongruous items were stacked together amongst packing cases and cardboard boxes. In a corner containing a sink and lavatory I also noted, apart from shelves of books, a bottle of sake and another of whisky, a broom, a pile of magazines dating from the 1960s, a piano covered in red and gold ruffled material on which perched a toy seal, two African dolls with bones through their noses, a Spanish doll in a glass case and an old hospital stretcher. The lavatory boasted a seat cover labelled 'Playboy' and a panel of buttons which I dared not touch in case they boosted me into space or, at the very least, provided a douche and blow dry.

Over breakfast the Reverend explained the reason for his wife's grief. Their only son, a dutiful and conscientious boy in his first year at university, had stopped eating two months before. Now he had been admitted to hospital. The prospect of inheriting the temple had caused his despair. 'Can't he do something else?' I asked, amazed to discover number eighteen in line suffering from a Western ailment like anorexia nervosa. The Reverend did not bother to answer; his son had appeared to understand the situation clearly enough. The only alternative to taking over the temple was suicide. Mrs Yamamoto apologized for 'surrounding you with tearful faces'.

During the morning, elderly Japanese arrived to celebrate the temple's main festival of the year, the traditional Japan that I had come to see. The congregation sat on tatami mats covering the temple floor. The old women had brown faces and wore shirts and trousers in faded prints. The old men, many with shaved heads, knelt straight-backed through the service. It was unseasonably hot. The wooden screens which formed the walls of the temple had been pushed back. A warm wind rattled the slates above my head on which were written prayers for the dead. The light shed by the altar candles flickered over the statue of the Buddha, surrounded by chrysanthemum and sacks of rice. On either side the Reverend and his brother-in-law knelt chanting. They wore robes of black gauze over white kimono. A novice priest, facing the altar, knocked together two sticks in time to the chant. The service commemorated friends or relatives who had died that year. Two old women cried quietly into handkerchiefs.

I returned to the house. In the hall women knelt on the floor preparing dishes of food for the eighty parishioners staying that night. They were so old and bent that they looked as if they had grown into that position and could not with ease hold any other. The kitchen took on a backstage atmosphere as the priests left the altar for a break. The Reverend complained of 'letting off steam' under his robes. He stripped to his vest and joined us at the kitchen table laden with presents of food and drink from parishioners. The novice priest, eating a strawberry, explained the difficulties of banging two sticks together. 'It takes years of practise,' he assured me. He had a shaven head and an attractive, gleeful face. His jokes made even Mrs Yamamoto smile. His father owned a temple in Wajima which he would eventually take over. His wife also came from a temple family as did Mrs Yamamoto. 'My father, brother and husband are all priests,' she said. 'Well, it's better. You know what you are getting into.'

The brother-in-law introduced me to his wife. She wore a purple dress with a boutonnière on her breast and inquired if I had been on the Orient Express. Did passengers wear black tie all day, even, for example, at breakfast? She and her husband planned to spend two weeks in Europe. As this seemed 'an awfully long time', they had decided to break it up with a journey on the famous train. They were busy buying a new wardrobe, the main purpose, it seemed, of the trip. The brother-in-law had just acquired a black tie from the local department store. Could I please explain about cummerbunds? Just then, a loud drumming erupted from the temple. Hastily the priests finished their beer, pulled on their kimono and returned to work.

That night after the parishioners had fallen asleep on their futons the Reverend and his wife questioned me. They knew nothing about anorexia nervosa. Japanese newspapers and magazines, unlike their British counterparts, never addressed the subject. I mentioned that a member of my family had the disease. The Yamamotos exchanged glances. Were these things discussed in the West, they asked? Did they not have friends with similar problems, I returned? Their faces grew anguished. Mrs Yamamoto seized the dictionary from her husband, looked up something then pushed the page at me, her fingernail digging a line beneath the example given in the dictionary: 'Mental illness is hereditary'. She fixed her eyes upon my face and said, 'My daughter has reached the age when she can expect to marry. If people heard of my son's illness, no one would marry her. We have told no one.' I stared in stupefaction, started to contradict her then lost heart. Mrs Yamamoto regarded me sadly. 'You live in a more open society, don't you?' she said and got up to make more tea.

Before going to bed, I wandered outside and climbed the steps to the temple. Two huge paper lanterns hung outside the doors. I paused beneath them. They cast a soft and magic light. Before me stretched a scene from old Japan; the courtyard, the twisted fir tree, the fire bell and, beyond, the narrow winding lanes with their wooden houses and open gullies. This was the idyllic view of rural Japan held by many Japanese who live in cities, like my neighbour Mrs Abe. They appeared to ignore the robustness which made it so attractive and the personal sacrifice which has allowed it to last so long.

On my return to Tokyo I found my attitude to Japan had changed. No longer could I enjoy its benefits as an outsider. I had entered in too deep. I was beginning to understand exactly how much happiness it cost to produce such a happy society.

9

When I returned from my stay in the temple, Midori greeted me excitedly. We were having a drink in a building whose owner had imported Florentine artisans in order to create amidst the sprawl of modern Tokyo the illusion of a Renaissance palace. Charlie and Midori had found the perfect plot of land for their house. It lay between an orange grove and a forest, overlooked the sea and was only an hour away by train from Tokyo. She said, 'We joked because I wanted the sea and Charlie the mountains and now we have both. So lucky we think.' Charlie explained that they were calling on the seller the next day. 'Why don't you come?' he asked. Letters from friends in England were filled with tales of buying a house in the country. Intrigued to see the outcome of this very English activity in Japan, I agreed.

After admiring the plot, we climbed the hill to a box of a house made more forlorn by an empty golfish pond. The seller was in his sixties, had been brought up in Taiwan and understood English even though he refused to speak it. He fixed a cigarette in a carved holder and mentioned an exorbitant figure. Charlie offered to buy half the plot. The seller sucked on the holder, 'I'll reduce the price if you use the company I suggest to put in your water supply.' Charlie shook his head. 'We intend to be in charge of our own destiny,' he stated in rather high-flown Japanese. The seller looked astonished. This very Western sentiment, like large houses and big cars was, as we soon found out, a luxury that few Japanese can afford. 'That's not how we Japanese do business,' warned the seller.

The sale went through. Charlie and Midori drew up house plans and arranged to meet the local carpenter. I was staying with them when he arrived. About fifty-five, he was tall with a crew cut and protruding stomach, 'a bit like Yogi bear, don't you think,' whispered Midori to me. She sat him down with a beer in a corner while we finished eating supper. After a moment he got up, crossed the room and stood watching us while sipping his drink. 'What's the matter?' asked Midori. 'Don't mind me,' said the carpenter, staring at Charlie. 'Excuse me but you are making us uncomfortable,' said Midori. The carpenter shook his head in wonder. 'This is the first time that I have come so close to foreigners. I've never seen them eating with chopsticks before. No, don't stop. Its very interesting, isn't it?' As Charlie remarked later, 'We were like wild animals in the zoo except that he wanted to get in the cage with us.' The carpenter warned them to check if the road below their property was public or private as it led to the reservoir from which the house got its water. 'It's a public road. We have already checked,' said Charlie impatiently. 'Really?' said the carpenter.

The next morning we called on the estate agent who also acted as Charlie's solicitor. To Charlie's concern over a conflict of interests, the agent had replied stiffly, 'Well that's how we do it in Japan.' The agent admitted that the road in question was in fact private. 'You told us that it was public,' said Midori. 'Well, it is public, up to your house,' amended the agent. Midori asked why he had not informed them of this before the sale. 'You didn't ask,' he said.

Next we stopped in the Town Hall for a plan of the area. Hand drawn and over a hundred years old, it proved as baffling as the estate agent. Boundaries stopped and started at whim. Midori explained that the Town Hall had always depended on farmers to supply a plan of each area. Like all Japanese they preferred to leave everything as vague and inaccessible as possible in order to give themselves an advantage in a deal. 'Is there no concept of free information here?' exclaimed Charlie bitterly as we examined the map with an official. Midori pointed to a line across their road. The Town Hall official sucked his teeth and said, 'It could be a boundary but then again not. Maybe the cartographer's hand slipped?' he added helpfully.

Charlie and Midori were just contemplating life in a house with no running water when they received a letter from the seller. He insisted that Charlie now buy all the land and not just half. He produced a confidential memo from Charlie to the estate agent to prove his point. When Charlie refused, the seller issued threats. Charlie took, for Japan, the very unusual step of hiring a lawyer who told him the seller was affiliated to the mob. Said Charlie, 'That's all we need, a gangster up the road who hates us.'

When Charlie rang the estate agent back he was told the man was out, then on holiday and finally, 'rather poorly'. A phonecall from the lawyer forced the agency to admit that he had been transferred to another part of the country for 'misrepresentation'.

It was at this inauspicious moment that Charlie and Midori held the traditional land blessing ceremony. They cleared a square metre of land, placed four bamboo stakes at each corner decorated with strips of white paper cut into zigzags. As we waited for the priest to arrive an old man in baggy workman's trousers came down through the trees towards us. He pointed to the road which had already caused Midori and Charlie so much trouble. 'The six families who live on this mountain laid this down. We think you should make a contribution.' 'When did that happen?' Midori said looking at the pot-holes. The neighbour admitted it was ten years previously, 'but you still have to pay and you owe me ¥400,000 [£2,400].' Midori asked what for. 'Everyone pays me that each quarter. I look after the properties around here, prune the trees, pick up the leaves, that sort of thing.' Charlie thanked the old man and turned him down. The old man stared at us, flabbergasted, then began to shout. 'You can't possibly say such a thing. You are new around here. If you want happy relationships with your neighbours you'd better pay, otherwise. . .', here his voice went quiet and sinister, 'I can't guarantee what might happen.' I glanced up. 'The priest has arrived,' I said with relief.

A Shinto priest wearing a black conical hat and fold upon fold of splendid, different brocades stepped from a modest sedan. He prepared a special altar on which he laid fruit, vegetables, fish, sake and salt. He then emitted a loud 'Oi' for sixty seconds in order to catch the god's attention. On the god's arrival, Charlie, Midori, their lawyer, the carpenter and I sipped the sake then, in turn, picked up a shovel, stuck it into a fresh pile of earth and turned it slowly before sprinkling it with salt.

Afterwards the carpenter invited us to his house to celebrate. As we were leaving four or five men and women hailed us from the road. They bowed, introduced themselves as neighbours and said that they were in a difficult position. For years they had been paying the old man protection money. 'He has never once pruned our trees!' Worse, the old man had told them that only he could get permission from the company to lay their water pipes to the reservoir. He had taken their money and lain the pipes illegally. The company had found out and was threatening to sue them. 'Why are you telling us?' asked Midori. They explained that one of their children had heard Charlie ordering the old man to leave. Charlie was a foreigner and he used a lawyer. 'We've never heard of anyone doing that before.' He did not have to do business the Japanese way. He could stand up against the old man. They begged him to take the drastic action of 'forming a committee and putting a stop to it'.

Bemused I turned to get into the carpenter's vehicle. I had expected a truck. Instead I found him seated in the latest, most expensive BMW. 'It's cheaper than putting money in the bank,' explained the carpenter. After dinner we all got drunk. The carpenter played 'some mean jazz' on the stand-up piano which took up half the sitting room. The carpenter confided to Midori, 'I've always hated foreigners. I never thought in my life that I would speak to one, much less get drunk and have a good time together!'

The carpenter's wife was a small, dumpy woman who ran a craft centre next to their house. 'Father and I are always together,' she said complacently about her husband to me in the kitchen. 'Sometimes I have a game of tennis. If he returns and finds the house empty, he's in a bad mood for hours. He wants me with him all the time.' Back in the sitting room the devoted couple got in a fight over who understood Midori better. They were fond of her and felt for her position. The carpenter explained to me, 'When I first met Miss Midori I thought she talked too much.' His wife said, 'I had to point out why you speak all the time. Mr Charlie's Japanese is very good but not quite good enough. Miss Midori has to do all the talking.' The carpenter interrupted, 'That's just what I said. In Japan it's normally the husband who deals with this kind of thing but in this case Miss Midori has to do the negotiating and organizing, all the man's work. I think to myself, "she's such a poor, skinny, little thing, I must help her".' Here he announced that he intended to solve the problem of the water supply. None of us believed him.

A month later he submitted a letter with the certified 'chop' or official seal of the company and a bill to Charlie. The letter gave permission to lay the pipe. The bill included a bribe and a night out in Tokyo. Charlie was stupefied. 'Only in Japan would a hick carpenter know how to do over a big city firm!'

Shortly after they had to go down to sign a contract with the carpenter. 'I have insisted they book us into a *minshuku*,' (the Japanese equivalent of a bed & breakfast) said Midori to me before she left. 'This is all costing Charlie far more than he expected.' They arrived at the carpenter's office and began to go through the contract. At five o'clock the carpenter's wife said, 'You must be hungry, why don't you go to your hotel?' Midori declined. 'We want to get this signed and finished,' she said firmly. The carpenter's wife went into a huff and walked out. 'I had to ask her to come back because she had the chop and nothing could be signed without her,' explained Midori later to me. In order to pacify her they agreed to go to the *minshuku* but instead of the modest establishment they expected, the carpenter drew up in front of an expensive *ryokan*. Midori was exasperated. 'We asked for somewhere cheap,' she said. The carpenter's wife was whispering to the *ryokan* owner. 'You are not thinking of treating us,' accused Midori. 'Don't worry,' soothed the carpenter's wife. 'The owner is my closest friend.' Mollified at the prospect of a discount, Midori and Charlie went to their room. While the owner was running the *onsen* for them, Midori asked her what the carpenter did. 'She didn't know and they were meant to be best friends!' The owner of the *onsen* served them an elaborate dinner in their room. As they finished, the carpenter and his wife arrived with the contract. Charlie shook his head. 'How could we argue over costs? We knew they were paying for us and those sort of places cost about £300 a head!'

Shortly after Midori had recounted this episode to me, my husband suggested we take them both out to dinner to celebrate their engagement. They arrived looking strained and barely talking to each other. The newspapers were full of articles on corruption amongst Japan's top politicians and businessmen. Charlie explained to my husband, 'It's not just them. Corruption permeates every aspect of life here. Even buying a house is a perilous activity. We are talking about death threats now.'

Over dinner, Charlie and Midori grew increasingly gloomy. Their other problems had proved beyond even their carpenter. Charlie said, 'I wanted to resolve things in a rational manner. Instead we have made two bitter enemies.' The seller's anger remained unabated and that month the neighbourhood committee, emboldened by Charlie's attitude, intended to stop paying protection money to the old man. Charlie said sadly, 'It's all so vague. The law is unclear even to our lawyer and his speciality is real estate. I am afraid the seller will do something menacing. He won't sell the rest of the land to us because he knows he can get a higher price for it once we have built our house. Japanese and Westerners have different attitudes to a stretch of wilderness. We are attracted, they are repelled. No Japanese wants to be the first to build. Our house will reassure them and make the spot that much more enticing. So we'll be stuck with neighbours. . .'

Midori had taken Charlie's criticism of Japan personally. She declared, 'I too am in an impossible situation. Charlie doesn't understand why we must pay protection money. I am caught in the middle. I have to explain what Charlie wants and then explain to Charlie what he should do. It's not enough to say he should speak better Japanese. It's the whole Japanese mentality that he must understand. I have to deal with the lawyer, the seller, the real estate agent, all men in their fifties and sixties who look down on me because I am a woman. I have no authority yet I have to give the orders!'

To pacify her, Charlie said, 'Well, we do have one nice neighbour whose hobby is photography.' He had invited them over and sent Midori into the kitchen in order to show Charlie some pictures of naked adolescent girls, 'man to man so to speak,' said Charlie. 'At least he was normal and friendly.' Far from diverting Midori, this story only angered her further. 'It was not like that at all,' she exclaimed. 'That is stupid, Western interpretation of events. He was not trying to get rid of me. He showed me the same pictures later. How can you have understood it that way?' We went outside to put them into a taxi, Midori still berating Charlie.

A month later we found them in a nightclub on a Saturday night. Charlie admitted they had given up on the house. 'We were arguing all the time.' He had sold the land back to the seller. 'I mean, look what a mess we had got into and we hadn't even started building.'

Charlie's disenchantment with Japan coincided with my own. Whatever I felt about the country before, I was still an observer. Pregnancy changed all that and gave me a new perspective. Pregnancy finally enrolled me into the Japanese system. The consideration I had first received proved shortlived. Then I had been looked on as a foreigner first, a pregnant woman second; now I was just pregnant. The pregnant woman joins the ranks of the handicapped and the aged. She discovers how a society treats its meek. In Japan they get short shrift. The Japanese seem to view kindness rather like Christmas lights, only to be turned on at the appropriate time. Good deeds are never wasted on strangers or in public places.

I first noticed this on the underground. Each compartment reserves six seats for the aged and the infirm. These were always occupied by middle-aged businessmen. They never moved and no one asked them to. The frailest old lady, the woman clutching a child and I were all left to sway at our peril. My complaints shocked Mrs Abe. 'Our businessmen are so tired!' she exclaimed. 'They are not being unkind, they are just ignoring you.' I said that was worse. She remonstrated, 'Oh no! They are too embarrassed to give you a seat and are waiting for the right moment.' I wondered when that might be. She said, 'Ask them just as they are getting off. That is always a good time.'

Mrs Abe was expressing a general sentiment. Japanese society lavishes its attention on the male; everything is done to soothe his existence. He passes from wife to secretary to bar girl in an endless round of solicitude. Westerners receive similar treatment which is why many find Japan a delightful place. This was now a closed world to me. Pregnant women are expected to get on and bear it.

A Japanese girlfriend went into labour around midnight. Her husband dropped her off at the hospital. 'See you in the morning,' he said cheerfully. It was her first baby, the hospital understaffed and her mother still in the countryside. She had the baby on her own but for a distracted midwife who popped in from time to time. By nine o'clock the next morning her husband still had not telephoned. Her patience finally at an end, the new mother asked the midwife to ring his office and inform him he had a daughter. 'His office!' said the midwife, horrified. 'Are you sure it's all right to disturb him there?'

Japanese society is still primitive enough for pregnancy to be a purely female concern. No doubt this would delight the authors of pregnancy books. They extol primitive societies where women are in charge of the 'birthing experience'. They should have joined me in a Japanese *onsen* with twenty Japanese old ladies, all of us naked, when we went on the Kobokan's annual visit to the countryside. The *onsen* was in the open air. We lay back in the hot water and gazed across the valley to a small, lumpy mountain covered with bamboo and fir trees. 'So why aren't you wearing ankle socks?' asked Mrs Komita. 'All Japanese wear socks when they are pregnant.' 'Don't your legs get chilly?' demanded her friend. I murmured that outside it was ninety degrees and humid. 'Socks keep the baby cosy and warm up your muscles for the birth,' said Mrs Komita severely to me. 'She doesn't bind her stomach either,' supplied the friend who had watched me getting undressed earlier. This stunned the occupants of the *onsen*. Japanese women always bind themselves, they informed me. Binding ensured the baby remained small. 'That way it comes out easily and does its growing after it is born,' they explained patiently. It also helped the mother's figure added Mrs Komita. Two old ladies not part of our group stared at me dubiously. 'She's so large. Do you think she ever had a figure?' whispered one to the other.

Afterwards we walked around the local museum. Mrs Komita soon got bored and returned to the absorbing topic of the pregnancy. 'But why are you so big?' she asked. I explained that my husband was a large man with a big head and broad shoulders but here Mrs Komita interrupted, 'and big down there, I'll say!' she exclaimed, whacking me between the legs with the museum brochure.

Pregnancy also brought me up against Japanese medical practices. Japanese display a slavish attitude to those in authority. Doctors, like middle-aged businessmen and teachers, are respected and coddled. They exert their power without question, interfering in every aspect of their patient's life. One forbade make-up during my first trimester. Another, in the heat of summer, warned me against chilling my body by eating too much cold food or washing up in cold water.

Doctors think as little of women as the rest of Japanese society. Startling statistics reveal a certain carelessness about a woman's life once the baby is born. Although the Japanese infant mortality rate is the lowest in the world, the maternal mortality rate tells a

173

different story. In 1986 it was the second highest amongst the developed countries, 13.5 Japanese women died in childbirth per 100,000 live births compared to 7.2 in America and 6.8 in England and Wales. Japanese are often accused of behaving badly to foreigners. Foreigners should take comfort. It is nothing to how they treat each other.

Ignorant of this I rang a hospital consultant for an appointment. The nurse said, 'Japanese doctors don't make appointments. You just have to wait.' I asked for how long. 'Three or four hours,' she replied cheerfully. I explained that I worked. She told me to try coming first thing.

I arrived at eight thirty the next morning. The hospital fees had led me to expect the Japanese equivalent of Harley Street. It could not have been more different. Instead of settling into an easy chair or a back copy of *Vogue* I joined fifty pregnant women slumped on benches in a corridor. Some had produced picnics and were feeding their children. Others sat knitting and gossiping with their mothers. Husbands, it seemed, had sensibly refused to come. I waited for an hour then walked to the top of the queue. The consulting room was as crowded as the corridor. Nurses running back and forth hurried me with assembly-line efficiency from a changing room to a row of curtained cubicles and on to an examining table. A doctor was making his way from patient to patient, his every comment audible to the entire room. One woman had a husband with a dismal sperm count. Another appeared to be suffering from genital warts. This proved riveting stuff until I remembered my own problem. Hastily I sat up. The nurse entered, pushed me down and drew a curtain firmly across my stomach. I stared at it in astonishment. On the other side of the curtain, hidden from view, the doctor and his students gathered around my legs. I felt the examination begin. Just as I began to wonder if a gang bang might not be preferable, the nurse returned. 'Why are you so upset?' she asked. I pointed out that an unknown number of men were examining my body. She looked puzzled. 'But they can't see your face,' she assured me.

The nurse then explained the doctor would spend five minutes talking to me. 'He spends five minutes with all his patients so please do not ask questions,' she frowned at me. 'You foreigners always want to question doctor. That is not the Japanese way.' Mindful of the nurse's instructions I got straight to the point. What about pain relief, I asked. This seemed not the Japanese way either. 'I tell my mothers to get on and bear it,' said the doctor. 'Pain makes you love the baby more.' I said if I hit him on the nose would he like me more? He sighed, shook his head and advised me to improve my attitude 'for the baby's sake. We Japanese believe an angry mother makes for a difficult delivery,' he added.

The following week we received a letter from the consultant. I had forgotten to send him a present. 'Everybody does,' said Mrs Abe when we asked her advice. Would a bottle of whisky do, I wondered? We had already paid his fee. She explained the consultant expected a gift of at least £500. The year before she had given her surgeon £1,500 in order to ensure good treatment. 'So it's a bribe,' said my husband. She shook her head vehemently. 'There's no bribery in Japan,' she insisted. We sent a box of shortbread instead.

It was perhaps fortunate the consultant and I did not see each other again. He failed to reach the hospital in time for the birth and so, nearly, did I. A Tokyo traffic jam almost forced me to have my son on the express way. 'We have stopped outside an animal hospital,' my husband remarked hopefully at one point. When we finally arrived half a dozen midwives took charge of me with kind efficiency. They gave me a shiatsu massage to relieve the pain and hurried me to the delivery room. Just as we entered, one gasped, 'You have not changed your slippers.' The delivery room, it appeared, required different footwear. Everything stopped while I shuffled out of one pair of slippers and into another. After that, it was too late to climb on to the delivery table. I gave birth standing up over a red plastic bucket but shod, at least, correctly.

My ordeal with Japanese procedure did not end there. Two days later I found myself once again sitting in line with some forty Japanese mothers. This time we wore nightgowns, a bath cap and a pair of sterilized plastic slippers. Newborn infants sucked away at us. The bathcap and slippers reflected the hospital's obsession with cleanliness. The hospital only permitted mothers to hold their children in this one corridor at feeding time. Before we could touch our baby we had to change our footwear, cover our hair, remove any watches and scrub our hands and arms. Otherwise babies were confined to a nursery with a glass wall in front of which friends and relatives gathered during visiting hours. The mother asked for her child, a nurse wheeled up the cot and everybody exclaimed and video-taped through the glass.

All the other mothers wore flannel nightdresses and their hair in plaits. They stared disapprovingly at my lace négligé. It was hard to imagine any of us as sex objects, however briefly, nine months before. Nurses walked up and down massaging engorged breasts. Women closed their eyes and submitted with only the occasional grimace of pain. At my turn I screamed, begged for aspirin and burst into tears. 'Is it so different in the West then?' demanded the exasperated nurse. I stared at the line of mothers recalling the treatment we had received, its lack of empathy, pain relief or privacy. I imagined their future with a child in a tiny apartment, an absent husband and no system of health visitors or even baby-sitters. Some would not go to a cinema or a restaurant for the next three years. Many, to the despair of the Japanese government, would refuse to got through the process again. 'Very different,' I replied without hesitation.

When I wrote about my experience for a British magazine I received a letter from a *grand dame* of Tokyo society, famous for her style and her perfect English. The letter itself rather than its politely expressed criticism puzzled me. She had written on a scrap of computer paper lacking even the most basic formalities like a heading or a date. That week I met her at an embassy dinner. I mentioned that she already knew me under my maiden name. For a moment she lost her poise. 'I never expected to meet you on an occasion like this,' she said, staring incredulously. I asked Mrs Abe for an explanation. She said, 'We don't think much of journalists in Japan. They are rather low on the social ladder.' I pointed out that in Britain we use the same stationery whether sending a letter to a duke, the bank manager or even a journalist. 'Really?' said Mrs Abe in her I-don't-believe-you voice. 'A little bit too democratic don't you think?'

I had glimpsed Japan from the underside up, a highly unusual perspective for most Westerners. Mrs Kono took me even further. For her, lunch at the Kobokan was the social occasion of the week. Tiny with a permanently bent spine, she nonetheless took the trouble to wear kimono, apply white foundation and pencil-in half-moon eyebrows beneath a glossy wig. Twenty years before she had taken up traditional Japanese dancing. Now in her seventies she had achieved a modest reputation and even gave lessons. Her delicate appearance and refined manner set her apart from the other old people. I assumed she came from a better background. One week as I helped her into her shoes she invited me to tea.

Mrs Kono was a widow who lived with her son, his wife and their two children. She had turned the best room on the ground floor into her dance studio. It boasted a parquet floor and a large mirror. We sat on cushions while the daughter-in-law served us Japanese tea and passion fruit jelly. She was a big, loud woman whose jolliness did not seem impaired by a black eye. I asked about the pile of leather handbags against one wall. 'Oh, we make them upstairs,' said the daughter-in-law. 'Mrs Kono's husband began the business.' I looked at the old lady, smiling and nodding her head at me, with new interest. Traditionally only *eta* (or *burakumin*) work leather. I was having tea with a family of Japan's outcasts.

Burakumin, a euphemism for *eta*, meaning 'full of filth' or 'non human', were hereditary outcasts who traditionally performed jobs considered unclean in a Buddhist society: burying the dead, slaughtering animals, working in leather. Discrimination against *burakumin* was cruel and relentless. The law confined the *burakumin* to certain villages and forced them to wear marks of identification such as yellow collars. *Burakumin* were banned from shrines and temples. On maps of Japan the mileage accrued by roads running through their village went uncounted as if the land and the people did not exist. Japanese still routinely use private detectives to check they have not hired a *burakumin* or acquired one as a prospective son or daughter-in-law. Yet *burakumin* are Japanese. Nothing differentiates them ethnically from other Japanese.

The Kobokan stands in one of Tokyo's poorest districts which includes a *burakumin* community. They worked in the slaughter house which provided Oshiage's first factory with the animal fat to make soap. Discrimination forced many *burakumin* to join the *yakuza*. Over 80 per cent of *yakuza* members are made up of *burakumin* and those other outcasts from Japanese society, second or third generation Koreans.

Mrs Kono's father had died six months before the Great Kanto earthquake in 1923. His death left his wife and two small children destitute. They moved into a room above a sushi bar. Her mother took in piece-work making hat decorations. Somehow they survived. 'We really had nothing and were lucky to be able to stay together.'

The earthquake destroyed the stone storage rooms used by the sushi bar. Choking on the dust and the fumes from the fire, they fled to an open space by the river. It was crammed with 30,000 people. 'Go away, go away!' shouted the crowds, pummelling the terrified widow and her children. 'There's no room for you.' Here the daughter-in-law interrupted, 'Just as well. They all got burnt to a crisp by a fire ball shortly after!'

After the earthquake they moved into makeshift housing erected by the government. At the age of ten Mrs Kono started looking after other people's children. She strapped her neighbour's baby on her back then went on to another family to take care of the infants. 'Everyone had just about nine or ten children then,' she recalled. When I asked how much she got paid, she laughed. 'I never expected money. Sometimes they let me use the bath or gave me a little left-over rice. I was always hungry.' She admitted that until she married she had never tasted meat, fish or even an egg. She nodded contentedly at her daughter-in-law. 'Now I am so happy compared to then.' It was a sentiment I heard again and again from the Kobokan's old people. Free from the threat of starvation, war and harsh work they found their old age a time of peace and plenty. 'This is the best time of our lives,' they declared. I wondered what the average British pensioner would make of this.

Mrs Kono's brother, with all other work banned to him, went into leather like his father. After he had learnt the trade he taught his sister. Together they made purses in the shack they shared with their mother. I asked what they did to relax. She looked perplexed. 'We were cutting and stitching purses eighteen hours a day. When we were not working, we slept.'

Her brother introduced her to a young man also in the same trade who had known their father. 'You belonged to a tight-knit community,' I commented. Mrs Kono hesitated. 'We had no choice,' she said finally. Did she go through *omiae*, I questioned, the formally arranged introduction of potential marriage partners? The old lady shook with laughter. She said, 'That was not for the likes of us. No, we just fell for each other.'

Her life improved after the marriage. Her husband was a large, jovial man with entrepreneurial flair who took advantage of the new fashion for Western goods. He designed and made Western handbags with immediate success. Mrs Kono reminisced, 'We had just married and started a new business. It was my first taste of happiness.' Her daughter-in-law pointed out that she was still working over twelve hours a day. Mrs Kono put her head on one side, 'Yes but somehow it didn't feel so hard. We were earning good money after all.'

Between the wars the Japanese government protected the leather business. In the absence of cheap imports Mr Kono only had to work twenty days out of every month. He spent his free time 'out on the town', recalled his wife indulgently. When I asked if she did not get lonely at night, she looked shocked. 'Oh no, my mother was living with us and he always gave his family money first. Any extra he kept for himself.'

179

Sometimes he took her to an *onsen* for the weekend. Her face melted at the memory. After the children were born, they went too. By then the business had expanded. The Konos employed six or seven people and as 'we felt it wrong to go away on our own, we invited them as well. It turned into quite an expedition! My husband did the driving.' They had a car I asked in astonishment. 'The only one in the district,' said Mrs Kono proudly. After the war they were also the first family to own a television set. People came from all over the neighbourhood to watch.

Her daughter-in-law interrupted. 'You make it sound like a holiday camp. You forget how hard you worked. Former employees always bring that up when they visit us.' 'It was a holiday camp compared to my childhood,' reproved the old woman then added, 'but it did help that I knew the business.' I asked how she had fitted in four children. She explained that she worked up to the first labour pains. After the birth she spent a week in bed followed by two weeks of housework. Then she returned to stitching handbags. Her mother raised the children. She said, 'I always looked forward to that first week after the baby. It was my favourite period. I lazed in bed, the only time I ever did, and my mother cooked me something tasty to build up my strength.'

We went upstairs to see the workroom. It stretched the length of the top floor. Handbags in various stages of completion were stacked in neat piles on the tatami mat waiting to be cut or stitched with hand-operated sewing machines. At one end a man sat cross-legged, cutting out a pocket. Tall, smiling and moustached, he so resembled my image of Mrs Kono's husband that, for a moment, I thought I had stepped back in time. This was their son, it transpired, in the same trade but less successful. The high tariffs which had enabled the Konos to own the area's first television no longer exist. People are buying cheap imported bags. The business now provides merely an adequate living. As I left, the daughter-in-law presented me with a summer kimono patterned with wisteria and one of the most beautiful I had ever seen.

A different view of the Konos came from Mrs Abe some weeks later. We were having our monthly lunch, our numbers somewhat diminished by the recent political and banking scandals. Mr Tashiro and Mr Kobayashi had both been forced to resign.

Mr Abe had stopped to gossip about this outside my house. At the end of our street floated a spectacular apartment block with curved sides, sweeping balconies and a marble foyer. The bank had bought the entire edifice for the Kobayashi's retirement home. No expense had been spared. My daughter Gabriella and I had watched the garden's transformation in just two days from a muddy patch to a vision of lawns, fully grown trees, camellia bushes and spotlights. 'It's like a fairy tale,' said Gabriella as the German landscape gardener, flown over specially, oversaw the positioning of the final pink hydrangea. Each apartment in the building cost £4,000,000. 'We are only allowing close friends to buy them,' Mrs Kobayashi had remarked.

'Quite out of the question now,' said Mr Abe to me with satisfaction. The scandal had banished the Kobayashis to an obscure suburb. I said I felt sorry for Mrs Kobayashi, shut up with a man of implacable energy used to issuing orders and travelling the world. Mr Abe giggled. 'Apart from the presence of a husband, her life won't be that different,' he said. Mr Kobayashi had never taken his wife anywhere. Just before the scandal broke she had enjoyed a brief shopping trip to London. It was her first time outside Japan.

I asked Mrs Abe why Mrs Kobayashi and Mrs Tashiro no longer came to the lunches. 'They do not appear in public,' she said. I pointed out that after a year of lunches we hardly counted as public. 'In Britain we don't stop seeing friends just because they are in trouble,' I added mischievously. Mrs Abe looked at me oddly but both ladies attended the following lunch. Mrs Tashiro had not been to the hairdresser and drank too much. Mrs Kobayashi still interested herself in everything and was deferred to by everyone. To my surprise the conversation returned again and again to corruption scandals. Mrs Abe could not leave them alone. She even brought up the house at the end of the road. 'Empty now I see,' she said with a rudeness typical of well-bred Japanese.

The ladies then discussed who to blame for the present scandals.

Naturally they did not put it down to the veniality of the Japanese in general or Mr Kobayashi or Mr Tashiro in particular. Whom they did hold responsible took me some time to work out. The ladies referred repeatedly to 'people from that background' in hushed tones. At first I thought they meant the Ministry of Finance. Finally I exclaimed out loud, 'burakumin!' The ladies started then frowned at me as if I had used a dirty word. They continued to employ every kind of euphemism as if the truth might conjure up a 'non-person' ready to spring out and attack us from behind Mrs Abe's plush sofa.

These upper-class ladies feared and hated the burakumin. Mrs Abe explained that before the war burakumin lived in designated areas. 'We knew who they were by their address.' This changed under the liberalizing effect of the American occupation. Burakumin escaped into the cities, acquired an education and even joined companies. 'But however high up the corporate ladder they climbed, however successful they became, they never forget their origins,' intoned Mrs Abe. Mrs Kobayashi broke in with a criticism often employed by anti-semites. 'They cannot be trusted. Their first loyalty is to each other.' Mrs Tashiro said in her soft voice, 'They are to blame for the trouble in the banks today. When they became branch managers, they lent billions to their friends.' By this she meant their fellow burakumin in the yakuza. She could not say so because 'yakuza' is another term most Japanese avoid using.

The other ladies murmured in agreement. Mrs Tashiro said her husband proposed to do something to save the situation. We all looked at her expectantly. He was going to Osaka the next day, she continued, to lecture a group of bankers. He did not propose to admonish them for incurring billions of yen of debt. He had a far more vital agenda: how to recognize and sack their burakumin employees. The Japanese had created a chimera which haunted them more effectively than any reality.

I left the lunch puzzled as to why members of the establishment should be afraid of a woman like Mrs Kono who had never tasted an egg before she married. The answer lies in the Japanese obsession with groups. A group, as I myself had discovered, provides security and happiness to its members. But no group exists in a vacuum. A passion to belong goes with an equal passion to exclude. The Japanese, masters of the group mentality, have long exploited this. For hundreds of years the *burakumin* performed a vital function: they were the outsiders. Without them the Japanese as a group could not exist. It is the same in Japanese schools. The infamous bullying that results in the murder of a number of children each year is often deliberately encouraged by teachers. For teachers know that nothing will instil a group sense in their pupils more effectively than the persecution of an individual. The teacher first picks on a child a little different from his or her classmates, one that is half foreign, has studied abroad or just comes from a more educated family. After initiating the bullying, the teacher tacitly encourages it, watching the cruelty unify an otherwise disparate class. For, like all people, Japanese are disparate. They are just unique in not wishing to be so.

Mr Sato had received an important promotion. The Kobokan decided to give him a party. Various people made speeches. One of the rock band raised a toast to 'Our Mr Sato, the only director in Japan who still sings with a rock band. Long may he continue to do so!'

Miss Fujino dressed in a blue crêpe dress cut fetchingly on the bias sat at the back of the room. She looked very ill and only moved with effort. 'I am concerned about your health,' she said glancing at my stomach. 'So good of you to come in your condition.' To this I could say nothing. Japanese often left me speechless either by their rudeness or kindness. I asked after Tachi, the rock band's drummer. I had expected him to be at the celebration. She looked pained. 'He is having a very difficult time. I fear he may have left us.' I fetched her a cup of green tea and asked her to explain.

Tachi was the youngest son of a *yakuza* couple. He had four brothers and a sister all of whom had been taken into care. His mother abandoned him as a baby. Both she and her husband were constantly in and out of prison for drugs and pimping. She specialized in procuring under-age girls. Tachi was placed in a foster family until the age of eleven when his parents suddenly recalled his existence. They discovered his whereabouts and began to harass the family with threatening telephone calls. Tachi's parents were affiliated to the Inagawa-kai, one of Japan's major gangs. The telephone calls reduced the foster parents to such a state that they took Tachi back to the Children's Guidance Centre. 'You never told us he was *yakuza*,' they remonstrated. 'We are too afraid to keep him.'

It is difficult for Westerners in Japan to grasp the terror *yakuza* inspire in ordinary Japanese like Tachi's foster parents. *Yakuza* have excelled at public relations. They have sold an image of themselves as brave upholders of tradition and protecters of the ordinary people or, as they call them, 'the people who walk in the sun'. *Yakuza* are able to perpetuate this myth for one reason: they control most of Japan's film and television companies and sponsor the lead actors and actresses. When an independent director made a film critical of the *yakuza* he received death threats. Finally thugs attempted to murder him in a car park. Westerners find extraordinary the supineness of many Japanese in the face of the *yakuza*; but they lack even the basic weapons with which to fight. They trust neither the police or the courts to offer protection, while the highest authority in the land, Japan's own government, is stuffed with politicians who have *yakuza* support.

No one dared explain the situation to Tachi. He understood only that his foster parents whom he loved had abandoned him. Three times he ran away from the centre. His foster mother opened the door to find him weeping outside and swearing, 'I promise to grow up into a good man, please keep me, oh please keep me.'

The authorities decided to send him to the Kobokan's Children's Home in Karuizawa. His real parents had already discovered the Children's Guidance Centre in Sumida-ku to which they were constantly making threatening telephone calls. 'The authorities thought he would be safe with us,' said Miss Fujino. A social worker drove Tachi to Karuizawa. As the car climbed up through the mountains, Tachi glanced over the edge. At the age of eleven, he later confessed to Miss Fujino, all he wanted to do was throw himself off that mountain and die.

He spent three years at the Children's Home. He settled down and developed into a talented athlete. Miss Fujino persuaded the Tokyo metropolitan government to pay for him to attend a famous athletics school in Tokyo. Tachi had just got a place on the football team when his mother turned up at the dormitory. His parents had finally tracked him down.

Yakuza are immediately recognizable by their clothes and their attitude. The over-made-up middle-aged woman pacing up and down the room swearing and demanding to see her son inspired shock, repulsion and fear in Tachi's classmates and teachers, never mind himself. The school got rid of her and bundled him back to the safety of Karuizawa and the Children's Home. 'But what is my background, what is my background?' he kept on demanding.

I interrupted to ask why Tachi's parents were so desperate to contact him. 'Power,' said Miss Fujino. The family operated as a unit. The more family members involved, the more power it wielded. 'That's the only reason they want him,' said Miss Fujino. 'For that they are willing to ruin his life.'

Now that the parents knew about the school the authorities had to concede to their demands. Miss Fujino set up an appointment at the Children's Guidance Centre in Sumida-ku. 'They still did not know about the Children's Home in Karuizawa and we did not want them finding out,' she explained. I tried to imagine this small, delicate woman confronting a *yakuza* couple. She admitted, 'It started off badly. They were very angry and wanted their son. I tried to remain calm and hide my feelings. I treated them as very important people. Slowly they quietened down.' Miss Fujino insisted that they break off all contact with Tachi until his graduation at the age of eighteen. They agreed on condition she set up a meeting with their son. 'We had to comply. In Japan the rights of parents are stronger than the rights of children.' She fixed a date for the family reunion.

First she had to prepare Tachi. Miss Fujino said, 'We just explained to him in part what his parents did. He would have been too shocked otherwise.' She did not mention, for example, that his mother dealt in under-age girls. It might have been better if she had.

The Children's Guidance Centre in Sumida-ku held the meeting in their offices. 'Weren't you afraid?' I asked. By this time Miss Fujino's assistant, Tomo, had joined us. He explained the family had never stopped threatening to beat up and even kill Miss Fujino. They knew of Tachi's devotion to her. 'Her's was the hold they had to break.' He went on to point out that as Miss Fujino had not long to live, 'she is the only person able to deal with them, because she lacks all fear. They can't hurt more than the sickness.' Miss Fujino gave me one of her long, curling smiles and adjusted the cameo brooch at her throat.

Outside the Children's Guidance Centre, Miss Fujino saw an intimation of things to come. Tachi's family had arrived in a stretch limousine which now blocked the front entrance. 'It was the only car not in the car park so I knew it belonged to them,' remarked Miss Fujino with a grimace. She and Tachi walked into the room and were immediately surrounded by *yakuza*. His whole family had attended. Apart from his parents, his four brothers, their wives and his sister and her husband greeted him familiarly. Tachi's face went white. He had not expected this. The men all wore the distinctive punch perm and bomber jackets of the *yakuza*.

Tachi insisted that they did not contact him until after graduation. At this Tachi's mother, dressed in black with numerous gold chains, stretched out her arms to her youngest child. Tears streamed down her cheeks. 'I wanted to keep you,' she choked, 'but my health broke down and I had to give you up.' Tachi's face began to work. Pressing the advantage, the mother invited Miss Fujino and Tachi to lunch. Miss Fujino agreed and found herself bundled into the stretch limousine. 'Well,' she said with a very small smile, 'I was curious to see what they were like. They were, after all, the real thing.'

They sat around a circular table in a Chinese restaurant. The father was a big man with a thick neck. Jokes on Dad's power and greatness dominated the conversation. Tomo explained without irony that *yakuza* are the guardians of traditional Japanese values. 'In days gone by fathers enjoyed enormous respect,' he added.

Tachi's siblings had all grown up in children's homes before graduating to juvenile prison. When not praising Dad, they swapped stories on prison life and the escapes they had pulled off. They asked Tachi for his experiences. At first Tachi looked to Miss Fujino for help but their good-humoured inclusion of him proved irresistible. His football career impressed everybody. 'Please take care of him,' they begged Miss Fujino as they said goodbye.

Miss Fujino continued bitterly. 'They promised not to contact him but of course they did.' He was recovering from a sports injury in hospital when his family again turned up. This time they were more themselves and their easy, cruel assumptions and their aura of menace got to the boy lying in bed. He was very upset and later almost had a breakdown. Finally he ran away from school. Mr Sato persuaded him to move into the Kobokan and try for another school. Miss Fujino said, 'He doesn't know what he wants. He is nostalgic for his people but fearful of *yakuza*.' She explained that he dreaded letting down those who had helped him, by which she meant herself. He was also proud of having belonged to a first-class soccer team. 'That pride I hope will sustain him,' she said then she shook her head. 'Even if he does get into another school, he never knows when his parents will turn up and wreck his life. Just their appearance will do that in Japan.'

The week before she had consulted a lawyer specializing in *yakuza*. He prophesied that the boy would return to his family, 'but afterwards he just might come back to us. But for now they've got him.' She leaned back exhausted. Tomo looked at her then rubbed his eyes impatiently. 'You foreigners tend to glamorize *yakuza*,' he said. 'Well now you know the destruction they cause, even to their own families.'

187

I had not heard from Yuno, my gambler friend, for almost a year when a letter arrived enclosing the polaroid photograph taken of us at the Thai poker club. Nida picked it up off the kitchen table. 'What a happy couple,' she announced. 'You can see they are made for each other.' The gambler wrote, 'How is your business? I'm OK! If have a chance I'll take you dangerous area.' I rang immediately. 'A little busy now,' he said against a background of male laughter. 'Call you tomorrow.' But he never did. Some weeks later I found myself near the coffee shop which he had taken me to. Recalling the owner and his interest in South African politics, I dropped in.

The owner sat me down in the shade of a rubber plant. The coffee shop resembled a greenhouse which had seen better days. A gangster slouched in one corner listening to *The Marriage of Figaro*. The day's take lay in a wooden box next to the compact disc player. Chess and Go boards were stacked on top of a pile of *Newsweek* magazines.

Behind a counter the owner prepared Turkish coffee in a space the size of a cupboard. Yoshi was a small, wiry man in his forties with an oversized head, large mouth and pointed, Puck-like ears. He wore loose garments from Pakistan and spoke English which he had taught himself from listening to the BBC World Service. A short-wave radio hung above the counter. Unlike the majority of Japanese I had encountered, he was consumed with curiosity about the world. He was also a fascist. 'Democracy, equality, fraternity,' he pronounced the words as if they were an incantation of evil. 'I don't believe in that stuff. Certain countries, like certain people, are just naturally superior. We Asians are all behind China's stand against the USA's demands for political reform. We are delighted that someone is resisting the United States.'

Encouraged by my evident consternation, he emerged from behind the counter and sat down on a stool near my table. He continued, 'Democracy! Human Rights! What are they but an excuse for the West to interfere in other countries? They enable the West to take what it wants while claiming the moral high ground, just as it used Christianity a hundred years ago to seize

188

continents. You are merely dressing up colonialism in new clothes.'

Exhilarated to find myself in a dispute – Japanese normally detest controversy – I counter-attacked with a swipe at Confucianism. We then set to in satisfying battle, no generalization proving too broad for either of us, before a final spat over the Second World War. It was the first time I had discussed the war with a Japanese. As a foreigner, knowledge of Japanese atrocities taints one's view of the country. It is a shock to discovery many Japanese are both ignorant and unconcerned. In December 1937, for example, the Japanese army sacked the Chinese capital of Nanjing. According to evidence gathered by the Japanese war crimes tribunal, Japanese soldiers killed 200,000–300,000 Chinese civilians and raped 20,000 women. They bound people together in bundles and shot them or set them alight. They tied others to posts and used them for bayonet practice. They photographed themselves and their victims and sent the snaps to family and friends back home.

Over fifty years later the Japanese refuse to acknowledge this massacre occurred. It is as if the Americans denied they had dropped bombs on Hiroshima and Nagasaki (which killed the same number of people). Young Japanese know every detail on this subject but when you ask about the invasion of China they look blank. 'Don't they learn about it at school?' I had demanded of Mrs Abe. She said, 'Our history goes back so many centuries and Japanese children have to study all of it. By the Second World War, they have run out of time.'

Yoshi's view proved more straightforward. The right wing are against admitting to any atrocity let alone making apologies. He said, 'The West want to cripple us with guilt. You never hear about atrocities committed by the victors – only the losers. Why should we feel guilty? We were at war. When you are pursuing a military strategy anything is justified.' I recounted details. He fell silent. Finally he said, 'We should put the past aside.'

At that moment two American models entered the coffee shop. Yoshi greeted each warmly and offered the girls a slice of cheesecake which he had baked that morning. After he had served them, he returned to his stool. I said I had not expected to find foreign models in his coffee shop. 'They come here all the time,' he explained. 'I offer them special rates. I know they don't have much money.' I said, 'I thought right-wing Japanese detested foreigners.' He looked embarrassed, 'Well, a foreigner once did me a good turn. This is how I repay his kindness.'

I asked for another coffee. Yoshi told me he had attended a 'second rate' university after failing to get into Tokyo University, the Japanese equivalent of Oxbridge. As a student he had fallen under the influence of Yukio Mishima, Japan's foremost modern writer, who was also a right-wing nationalist. He followed the teachings of a Chinese philosopher, Wang Yang-Ming, who believed in action rather than study or observation. This action sprang from a refusal to compromise with the world's injustices and invariably led to a violent death. Mishima argued that his country had lost its spirit in pursuit of security and materialism. He yearned to take a stand and die for his ideals. Unfortunately no suitable occasion presented itself. In the end Mishima had to create his own. On 25 November 1970 he and a follower invaded the headquarters of the Eastern Defence Forces in Tokyo. The pseudo coup followed by their ritual suicide achieved nothing. As Mishima wrote a few months before his death, the sacrifice was all.

The man now serving me coffee had belonged to the inner guard of Mishima's Shield Society which he had created and trained as a symbolic force to protect the Emperor. Yoshi's best friend had joined Mishima on his mission. He had cut off Mishima's head, the traditional action of a retainer when his lord commits ritual disembowelment. He had then followed Mishima's example but without the benefit of anyone to put him out of his agony. 'Why didn't you join in?' I asked. Yoshi replied, 'They kept the coup to themselves. It came as a complete surprise.' When he heard the story he hurried across Tokyo to the headquarters where he found other members of the Shield Society seeking to discover what had happened. 'The police promptly

190

arrested us. In the corridors and lavatories of the police station we were all grabbing each other desperate for news.'

A member of the Shield Society went on to found a notorious right-wing organization which Yoshi joined. Its members still cruise Tokyo in black lorries decorated with the Japanese flag and blaring martial music. Sometimes the lorries stop, blocking the traffic while a man inside exhorts and deafens passers-by. 'That's democracy for you,' shrug the Japanese, if you complain.

These demonstrations have another more lucrative purpose. In Japan the right-wing extremist and the gangster are often one and the same. They hold the same beliefs and employ the same means. The lorries park outside office or apartment blocks and blast out embarrassing details about the companies or individuals inside until they are paid off. 'Do you receive money?' I asked Yoshi. He insisted they did not. He held equivocal views on his group's ties with the *yakuza*. Although he had befriended Yuno and at that moment a gangster was drinking coffee in his bar, 'when they asked me to provide protection to a top *yakuza* during a gang war, I refused.'

I remarked that Yoshi would be the first to suffer after a right-wing coup. 'They won't approve of you reading *Newsweek* or entertaining foreigners.' Yoshi laughed, shook his head and hurried off to take another order from the Americans. In the corner the gangster licked his forefinger then turned the page of a pornographic comic book. A pile of them lay next to the *Newsweeks*.

That evening I met Mr Abe exercising his falcon and his dog in the grounds of the nearby Medical Research Centre. Built in the 1920s, a decade when Japan admired and emulated all things Western, its ramparts, turrets and medieval windows towered above us. Wooden houses and Nissen huts dotted the overgrown grounds. From one shed came the smell of ether and a sudden bout of hysterical barking from the dogs kept inside for experiments. Medical students were playing on the hospital's two tennis courts.

191

My acquaintance with Yoshi had forced me to grapple with issues I had so far avoided. The war haunted me. Elderly Japanese blamed the military because of their 'imperfect understanding of the samurai code', as Japan's former ace pilot had told me. Officers, others claimed, had deliberately brutalized the Japanese soldier. Many committed atrocities in order to win acceptance from their comrades or relief from the cruelty of their superiors. At the end of the war disillusioned men on the boats home hurled their commanders into the sea. Others sought out officers in Japan and murdered them in front of their families.

Exasperated by my moral outrage an elderly British homosexual who has lived happily in Japan since the 1960s pointed out that it was not Japan but 'a Christian nation which implemented the concentration camps'. Nonetheless the hierarchical nature of Japanese society provides the environment and the occasion for cruelty. It is not something that ended or began in the Second World War. In schools, for example, it is acceptable for a teacher to lose his temper and wallop a child across the face. I knew one English woman married to a Japanese to whose child this had happened. She complained to the headmaster but the child begged her never to do so again. 'It only makes it worse,' he said. She told me bitterly that no one could understand Japan 'who hasn't put their children through the Japanese school system.'

When I recounted this story to Mr Abe, he murmured that he had received the same treatment at school 'if not worse'. The slightest misdemeanour earned 'a good slapping around the face'. In his last year, he had started a soccer team. As a matter of routine he humiliated the younger players, hit them, 'anything to get the boys to kick the ball.' He added, 'It worked. I created a very successful soccer team.' I stared with astonishment at the mild and eccentric Mr Abe now bending down to pull his dog's ears. I failed to imagine him raising his voice let alone using violence.

After the war he had joined a mountaineering club where he got clouted for not hurrying up the slopes, making camp fast enough or finishing his rice at mealtimes. I pointed out that people in the West managed to climb mountains without such inducements while no one would hit an adult for leaving his food. We had reached a piece of open ground and Mr Abe prepared his falcon for flight. He removed the hood and jesses. Coaxing and crooning over the bird, he raised his arm. We stood and watched it soar. Mr Abe said, 'Compared to the Westerner we Japanese are not strong. We have to make up in spirit what we lack physically. During the war we believed the only way to force our men to fight ferociously enough to overcome the Westerner was to brutalize them.'

Midori and Charlie's relationship mirrored my own confusion. The house had represented more than their friends realized. The failure to build it signalled the failure of their love. They sniped at each other continually. Each felt they had been let down not just by the other but all the other represented. Both had seen the affair as an escape from their background. Now they were back where they had started. Midori said to me, 'His family is so uncivilized. I don't want to live like a monkey in a tree.' It proved almost her last confidence. I had become irrelevant.

One evening in the Ginza, after visiting an elderly *mama-san* who had befriended me, I failed to find a taxi home. It was very cold. In a tent on the pavement a man was serving noodles to six customers seated around a kerosene heater. It looked warm and companionable. I bent down, pushed aside the flap and slipped on to the bench. As I slurped up *oden*, a soupy vegetable and fish stew, I heard the unmistakable voice of my neighbour. I peeped around the flap. Mrs Abe, wearing a dress decorated with metal studs beneath a mink coat, was standing at the crossing waiting for the lights to change. The youthfulness of her clothes amazed me but not so much as her companion: it was Charlie.

They stood apart and barely glanced at each other. Only I, hidden as I was with my head at waist level, could see Mrs Abe press her fingers lightly against Charlie's thigh before slipping them back into her pocket. Then the lights changed and they vanished into the crowds. I sat transfixed. I had never imagined Mrs Abe as anything but a middle-aged housewife. Then I recalled my first visit to her house and the question, 'What is your hobby, tennis, golf, or young men?'

The next morning found me again spying on Mrs Abe, this time from my kitchen window. She was engaged in the traditional early-morning activity of Japanese housewives, sweeping the pavement in front of her house. When she had finished, she fetched what appeared to be a vacuum cleaner, only this blew out air rather than sucked it in, and trained it on the leaves lying in the gutter. The leaves scattered then settled outside the homes of her neighbours. Mrs Abe nodded with approval at her clean portion of road, glanced at mine, leaf clogged and unswept, and went back inside.

Midori had grown secretive and taken to disappearing. I accused her of having an affair but at that she looked sad. Charlie was talking of returning to England without her. Late one night in a nightclub he described to me a weekend he had spent in Scotland on a recent holiday. He had gone on a walk with two couples. They had chatted, in that casual, incestuous manner of the English, of mutual friends and last year's parties. The conversation had left Charlie silent and furious. They had shown no interest in him beyond confusing Hong Kong with Tokyo. 'I wanted to say, "I am one of you. I belong too, you know,"' he added, hunching forward on a slab of exotic hardwood which formed the bar. Above us hung an ornate Florentine mirror. In its reflection I watched two men dressed as sumo wrestlers dance on a raised platform. Slowly they unwound their loin cloths, turned their backs on us and inserted a clutch of sparklers up their bottoms. A girl wearing a see-through kimono set the sparklers alight.

I turned back to Charlie. Moodiness emphasized his good looks. I pointed out that he had lived a long time abroad. The implications of this he could not accept. He wanted passionately to fit in to English society. He yearned to discuss London schools and houses in the country. I mentioned Midori. He tried to shrug her off but even now his eyes searched the mirror for a glimpse of her dancing in a red dress that left her arms and legs bare. 'Could an

English girl suit you as well?' I asked. He looked at me helplessly. His own insecurity with English society precluded a return with an older, Japanese wife. He loved her but he did not have it in him to love her enough. Behind us the fake sumo wrestlers had turned around and were now, very carefully, setting their pubic hair on fire.

Charlie's vacillation made life intolerable for Midori. One moment he asked her to come to England; the next he talked of their parting as a matter of course. Finally she came to me weeping. She wanted nothing better than to marry him. Charlie's unexpected love followed by his equally irrational rejection had undone her. At the same time Mrs Abe appeared strained and unhappy. I assumed that Charlie had started the affair in order to extricate himself emotionally from Midori. 'Why is your neighbour so rude to me whenever I visit?' asked Midori.

Charlie went on a series of business trips before his departure and I saw less and less of Midori. She had returned to her Japanese friends. Finally she invited me to lunch with her latest, a girlfriend of a famous Japanese architect.

I arrived first at the restaurant. The tables were full of Japanese women who had spent large amounts of money and time on themselves. They spoilt the effect the moment they hobbled, awkward with apology, to their seats as if society's restrictions had somehow fastened around their limbs. Midori and her friend, on the other hand, paused as they entered the restaurant like Western women. Yoko wore a man's suit and shook back a cloud of permed hair. They sashayed over to our table enjoying the nervous, disapproving glances from the other diners. A Western man would have found their confidence exciting. The Japanese saw in it a lack of respect and turned back to their lunch unimpressed. They found Peter Pan collars and lowered eyes infinitely more arousing.

During pudding, Midori brought the conversation around to a friend of Yoko's. This woman had started as a hostess at the age of fifteen but soon graduated into a high-class whore. 'She never wasted a moment on any man who was not well-born, famous and rich,' remarked Yoko. The eldest son of one of Japan's oldest and most eminent families fell so much in love with her that he divorced his wife and proposed. She was thirty-five, having a good time and unwilling to marry. 'She never found him remotely sexy,' confided Yoko, 'but her friends egged her on. After all she was not going to be young for ever and as his wife she would be treated like royalty.'

Before the marriage she had to undergo a transformation from bar girl to a member of the Japanese upper class. She emerged able to dress, behave and, most importantly, speak correctly. 'It was like learning a new language,' explained Yoko. To all appearances a lady, she agreed never to see her family again.

Her education failed in one respect. Yoko's friend had left school too young to have learnt enough Japanese characters to enable her to read. Yoko discovered this one afternoon when her friend tossed over a book. It was a novel by a famous author besotted with the former hostess. He had given it to her and now wanted an opinion. 'Please tell me what he says,' she asked Yoko.

She constantly feared discovery by someone from her past life. She and Yoko attended the same health club. Once they got into the lift with a *yakuza*. The women were wearing track suits with no make-up and their hair scraped back. The gangster peered closely at Yoko's friend. Suddenly he exclaimed, 'Holy shit, it's you! You have aged! I didn't know that you were living around here now.' Yoko's friend quickly lied about a husband and a nearby flat. 'She was mortified,' confided Yoko. Dressed up, sparkling with jewellery, she could escape detection. Her husband had even bribed the newspapers to silence. The most critical remark to appear merely stated that she had left school at thirteen.

Yoko shook her head. 'Still, she runs awful risks.' She charmed everyone and was always the centre of attention. Her husband was now dead and she took lovers at every opportunity, 'even foreigners'. Her latest wore a wig and owned one of Japan's largest construction companies. 'She's still a snob,' said Yoko. The two women paused to discuss whether the lover removed the wig in bed. Yoko finally admitted she had asked her friend who had remarked, "it's not his head that needs my hands!"' Midori snorted, 'What kind of sex do they have if he can keep his wig on?'

Midori and Yoko burst into laughter. Nearby businessmen stared, affronted. The waiter now served our coffee. Yoko and Midori moved on to discuss plastic surgery. I remained silent. I had listened to Yoko's account of her anonymous friend with recognition and horror. Finally I interrupted to beg Yoko to reveal the woman's name. Midori looked at me, her eyes hard and bright, 'Haven't you guessed? It's your neighbour and Charlie's new friend, Mrs Abe.'

10

'e are going bicycling,' said Mrs Goto excitedly. I
looked perplexed. It was the morning of my last
visit to the Kobokan. After six years of living on
and off in Japan I was returning for good to London. Mrs Goto
was describing the plans for my farewell party. Somehow I had not
imagined bicycling to be on the agenda. 'Bicycling,' Mrs Goto
repeated in English, 'you know, eating while you cycle!' I shook
my head. Mrs Goto had started taking English lessons once a week
in order to further our friendship. After trying without success
various pronunciations, she led me into the hall. Everybody
looked unusually formal. The old people had put on their best
clothes. Some of the old ladies had been to the hairdresser. Miss
Fujino wore a lace jabot and even the rock band were there in
shark-skin suits, their hair greased back. Japanese characters pinned
on to the curtains at the back of the small stage bid me farewell. In
the centre six tables had been pushed together, covered with a
tablecloth and spread with a magnificent buffet. Mrs Goto
explained that, in honour of my departure, we would be eating
'English style' or 'bicycling' from dish to dish, helping ourselves.

Half-way through lunch Mr Sato arrived fresh from his honeymoon. He had broken the news of his marriage some weeks
before. He said his fiancée was a school teacher aged thirty-nine
with her own interests. My husband explained, 'Of course he must
get married. He's been made director. He can't be a director and
not be married.' On my next visit to the Kobokan Mr Sato

admitted that the whole thing had been arranged. He appeared lacking in his usual ebullience. 'I've got flu,' he said when I pressed him. The old ladies were all delighted. We had spent many hours in the *kissaten* discussing Mr Sato's marriage prospects. 'She'll have to realize that she's marrying the Kobokan too,' said Mrs Goto.

The wedding was held in a church which took up one floor of a building overlooking a busy street. Mr Sato looked white and shaken as if the full force of Japanese society had gathered itself up and hit him on the head. 'Such a pity about the flu,' said Mrs Goto. From where I sat, I could see the bride waiting with her father to enter. She had a strong, intelligent face which in the privacy of the corridor beamed with pride. Once stepping with painful slowness up the aisle, she assumed the sorrowful expression considered suitable for Japanese brides. At the altar she sobbed.

At the reception afterwards we stood through thirty minutes of speeches, the sushi, sandwiches and cans of beer untouched before us. The new Mrs Sato's maid of honour recounted previous attempts by the bride to marry. 'She had completely given up hope when this offer came, as if from heaven,' she stated. Waiters hurtled around handing out glasses of sparkling wine for the toast. After that everybody fell upon the food. When I went up to congratulate the couple, I asked Mr Sato about his health. 'Oh I am quite recovered, really well in fact,' he said surprised by his own happiness. His wife squeezed her hands together with pleasure. Mr Sato's colleagues at the Kobokan presented him with two train tickets to a well-known beauty spot not far from Tokyo. 'Otherwise it would never have occurred to him to take a honeymoon,' they explained.

At the end of my farewell lunch, Mr Sato stood to begin the speeches in my honour. A social worker, much to my embarrassment, thanked me for giving her a true understanding of social work. Mrs Goto retold the *oshibori* story. Mr Sato recalled the landmarks of my friendship with the Kobokan after which Mrs Komita got up and planted herself firmly in front of me. She had been chosen to present the card inscribed by the old people and members of the Kobokan. Staring hard at me she said, 'Mrs Harriet has been coming every week to see us. She does us great honour. We have had some good laughs together. . .' here her face began to work, '. . .and I am going to miss her.' Thrusting the card into my hands she returned to her seat. She remained unusually subdued for the rest of the afternoon and left before the finish.

Only then, standing between Mrs Goto and Mr Sato, the faces of the old people smiling upwards, did I begin to understand what this departure would cost me. Like Charlie, departure concentrated my mind on Japan and what I had gained here. In England I would cease to be a foreigner. A visit to the drycleaner's would offer little prospect of adventure. The friendships that formed quickly and firmly against the alien backdrop of Tokyo would be unlikely to bloom over a London dinner table. The early hours would no longer find me in the nightclub district, stepping into a lift, choosing a floor and pressing a button for an extraordinary but safe experience. The sheer pleasure of life in Tokyo had come to an end. Japanese who have lived in London make the same complaint. London represents exotic freedoms. 'My wife and I go out together at night,' said one Japanese to me in awe. 'What will we do back in Tokyo?' For those who live abroad not belonging becomes a dangerous addiction.

As a woman I had seen a very different country to my husband. Japan had forced us to lead separate lives and we had made separate friends, mine, perhaps, more hard-won but more lasting. I had found myself in back-room Japan, unexpected and often unrecognizable from the myths I'd been fed. I had tried to judge it, but in the end judging a country is pointless. Japan is just different and therein lies its interest. It is the fascination of a people who are alien in even their most basic instincts. It is the formidability of getting to know them and, for me in the case of the Kobokan, of loving them. The effort had cost me so much that I feared, back in England, I would find I had left a great deal of myself behind; that in trying to love another country, I had become a traitor to my own, a foreigner in my own land.

After the lunch Mr Sato and Miss Fujino saw me off. Pale and in pain, she told me that Tachi had returned to his *yakuza* family. Japanese rarely touch each other but now I took her hand. She was the most extraordinary woman I had ever met and I doubted I would see her again. Mr Sato helped me out of my slippers then walked down the road with me. We said goodbye on a street corner. He paused, unsure how to express his emotions. Finally he said, 'You share the same attitude as Miss Fujino to social work.' It was, even I understood, a declaration of genuine affection and as near as he would ever come to making a personal remark.

Mrs Yamada also invited me to a party. Not so much a farewell as notice that she had recovered from her troubles and returned to her effulgent self. The chairman of a soft drinks company, and an old admirer of Mrs Yamada, held the event. She had invited an eclectic group of friends including the head cook from the Imperial Hotel, the chairman of the Japanese Critic's Association and a Japanese professor of Anglo Saxon who could not speak a word of modern-day English. Mrs Yamada, transcendent in kimono, was made much of. 'So sad you were here through my boring times,' she said to me as I bid her farewell. 'Now life will be much more interesting.'

Nida had decided to return to the Philippines to be with her family although she threatened to 'run away' if her husband proved less than doting. I also saw Yuno the gambler again but he had grown fat beyond recognition. It was outside the coffee shop which I continued to visit until my departure. He passed me without speaking. Yoshi confirmed it was indeed him. Yuno had lost all his money and even sold his car. This seemed a sadder end than any of his creditors could have devised. He still had enough to move from hotel to hotel. I asked from where he received money to exist. 'He is a friend of the common people,' said Yoshi, echoing the false sentimentality of every Japanese gangster film. I remarked that extortion was hardly a friendly activity. 'He gets it from professionals,' amended the coffee shop owner. He had withdrawn behind the counter to wash up. 'But what does he do for them?' I persisted. Yoshi disappeared into the fridge. The *yakuza* used the gambler to win money off the punters but he had failed. Lack of funds, I suspected, also accounted for his weight gain. He could no longer afford the amphetamines which kept him thin.

A few months before I left Yoshi introduced me to his wife. She was small and dumpy and appeared older than him. 'She knows all about traditional Japanese art and history,' he told me proudly and pointed to three of her paintings hanging on the wall. A potted gum tree hid the one I liked best. 'It should be spot lit,' I suggested. Yoshi scolded. 'That's a very Western attitude. We prefer it shaded.' His wife finished the sketch of me she had done while I was talking to her husband. It made me look like a witch.

Each time I returned to the coffee shop, Yoshi took up the argument where we had stopped the week before. The West both fascinated and repelled him. He resented the imposition of its moral and aesthetic standards. 'Japanese even use Western men to advertize their underpants,' he exclaimed. He berated Westerners for their sense of superiority with all the bitterness of a man who felt his own overlooked.

Our conversations grew more intimate. He recalled with pleasure fighting left-wingers during the student riots of the 1960s. 'I used to crack them on the head with a drain pipe. It made an excellent weapon. At weekends we went to rough areas like Shinjuku to practise on the gangsters.' I said it sounded very lively. Life as a coffee shop owner must be dull in comparison. 'Are you happy now?' I asked. To my surprise Yoshi said, 'Of course. I have the same philosophy and it keeps me happy. It always has and it always will.'

For him as for Mishima, happiness still came from living with the possibility of a violent death. Yoshi had been born into the wrong age to raise a rebellion and die for his beliefs as his heroes had done in the past. He scorned Mishima for faking a cause. Instead he climbed mountains. Every month he and a group of like-minded friends tackled perilous routes, 'always beyond our ability. We want to push ourselves to the brink.' A number had fallen to their death. Yoshi had retrieved the corpses, zipped them into body bags, then carried his former companions down the mountainside, 'half envious of their end.' Sometimes he spent the night on ledges where a single turn could send the sleeper hurtling into the depths. 'The danger makes me ecstatic. Can you understand that?' He shook his head. 'I believe no Westerner can. Westerners want life at any price.'

He always climbed with the same group which included a former left-wing revolutionary implicated in blowing up eighteen people in the 1960s. Mishima had grudgingly admired the left-wing students because they too were prepared to die for their beliefs. Yoshi said, 'We argue politics in the car all the way down but once you are hanging from a man's rope, it's no longer relevant.'

He told me the police still kept track of him. He gestured towards the pay phone. 'Even that's tapped,' he said. He complained about the effect this had. 'When I talk to my friend whose telephone is also bugged, we can hardly hear ourselves speak. Please tell your government to sell Japan some superior equipment. You have more practice in counter-espionage.'

I was just leaving the coffee shop after an invigorating argument when he suddenly retreated behind the counter. He said that he had fallen in love. All his friends had noticed. He had never felt anything like this before. Bewildered, I congratulated him. 'But its hopeless,' he said passionately. 'We both have families. She has children. There is nothing but unhappiness ahead.' I walked home in a daze. It was the strangest declaration of love I had ever received. It was also entirely in keeping with his philosophy. Yoshi had not wanted an affair or even a one-night stand; he had not even thought about it. He had wanted all or nothing. As all appeared impossible, it had to be nothing. The declaration had been his equivalent of the last stand taken by his heroes. He had deliberately destroyed his hopes even as he voiced them. Half a dozen conversations over cups of coffee were suddenly invested with an emotion far more profound than the circumstances. He expected never to see me again.

He reckoned without my vanity and obtuseness. Three days later I went back. He stared at me without speaking then withdrew behind the counter and began to cook furiously. The coffee shop was soon thick with the smell of curry. When I said something, he snapped at me. 'I'm busy. You have misunderstood the situation. Just because you are a Western woman you think all Japanese men are after you. I despise Western women and I despise Japanese men who fall for them.' He was now chopping onions with great vigour. After a final slice, he continued, 'I treated you differently because you came here as Yuno's friend. That was the only reason. That's why I talked to you. It's very irritating the way you always want to talk. I have to earn my living, you know. I can't spare the time. You are, after all, just a customer.'

I stared at Yoshi in stupefaction. I was fond of the coffee shop owner. Our differences had made me value our friendship as unique and precious. Two customers came in and he hurried over to them, roaring with laughter when one cracked a joke. As he prepared their coffee, I said, 'I understood what you said before but I don't understand this.' He banged sugar bowl on to tray and replied, 'You can never be an intimate of mine. You don't feel for music.' I looked at him flabbergasted. 'How do you know?' I said. Suddenly I got very angry indeed. I failed to understand Yoshi or his philosophy. I felt as if he had taken me up because I was a Western woman and rejected me for the same reason. I said, 'And what about you? Everything you believe in, I was brought up to hate and condemn.' He had come out from behind the counter and with deliberate cruelty I rose to my feet. I had always avoided standing near him. Now, looking down from at least four inches, I put the price of a coffee into his hand and left. It took days to get the smell of curry rice out of my hair.

After the revelation about Mrs Abe, Midori and I drifted apart. When Charlie left Japan for good, she moved back to her parents. We invited her to dinner but she had to leave early to catch the last train home to the suburbs. Sometime later I received a wedding announcement. Midori was marrying a Japanese. 'It's not an invitation,' I said, disappointed, to my husband. He reminded me that Japanese weddings, with their formality and interminable speeches, are better missed. When I learnt that she had given birth to a son, I invited her to tea with the child. She refused, explaining it meant taking a train and 'I can't travel with my son.' I pointed out that I took my young children on twelve-hour flights to England and back. Midori remained obdurate. 'I never go out with him. I don't know what he will do,' she said as if referring to a small wild animal. 'It could be so embarrassing.' In the end Gabriella and I went to her.

Midori and her husband lived in a suburb about an hour's commute from the centre of Tokyo. When she opened the door I barely recognized her. She wore no make-up or jewellery. Her glossy curtain of hair lay in a lifeless plait down her back. A pair of dungarees replaced her former Armani suits beneath which her body appeared to have shrunk and caved in on itself.

The apartment proved a further shock. It is impossible to understand Japanese society fully until one has been inside the small and claustrophobic homes they are forced to inhabit by the government's policy of keeping land prices artificially high. Midori's consisted of two rooms, each the size of the walk-in cupboard she had shared with Charlie when they lived together. She saw my face. 'We could have had something bigger if we had moved further out but we wanted to be close to the centre of Tokyo.' An hour's commute seemed hardly close but I said nothing. 'It's very sunny, isn't it?' she added hopefully.

She offered us something to eat. 'I've made a cake,' she said. I recalled her elaborate and delicious dinners and asked for a big slice. Without ceremony she pushed a wedge of sponge towards me. It had been prepared from a packet and tasted like cardboard. Gabriella built a wall out of hers.

Over tea I tried to resurrect our past pleasure in each other. It proved almost impossible. Midori was now a mother and a housewife. In the chameleon fashion of the Japanese she had succeeded in making herself like every other young mother in her

206

block. The new situation had called for a new persona and little of the old remained. She was evasive about her husband. I suggested they come to dinner but she shook her head, 'I think you would find him very boring. He's just a salary man.'

I asked how they had met. She looked embarrassed. Finally she admitted that after Charlie's departure, her parents had suggested that she marry. At her age the only chance of marriage lay with the services of a marriage broker. 'What about your television career?' I demanded. She explained that had come to an end. She said, 'I just got too old. Japanese like very young girls.' The confident, modern woman, the Japan of the future that I had seen in Midori, had lasted only as long as her youth. In the end it had proved as ephemeral as a drop of water in the summer's heat.

Midori explained that a suitable man had expressed interest in her photograph and they met for dinner. I recalled the restaurant. It boasted a Ladies floored and walled in black marble speckled with minute spotlights. Set in the marble above the lavatory roll, a miniature video screen showed *Casablanca*. The management also provided toothbrushes and scented toothpaste for those con-templating a love hotel. Midori was not thinking of love hotels. She was too busy erasing her Western mannerisms for the cute and docile ways beloved by the Japanese businessman opposite her. 'At my age you don't get many chances,' she said. That was the first and last time they went out to dinner together. She apologized for not inviting me to the wedding. She explained, 'We Japanese don't ask friends to weddings, just colleagues from my husband's office.'

I asked where they had spent their honeymoon. She blushed and offered to prepare more tea. Finally she admitted that they had gone to Maui, an island which we had visited together with Charlie and a group of friends. 'My husband chose it,' she said defensively. I remembered how she and I had sat on the beach and laughed at the Japanese honeymoon couples, self-conscious, immaculately dressed and silent. After that I could not bring up the past.

All the while her son played quietly in a corner. My daughter, bored and restless in the cramped space, began to hit him with a toy trumpet. I chattered about our children. Midori relaxed and grew animated. She slept with her son every night. 'It comforts him if he wakes.' 'How cosy for you and your husband,' I said politely. She shook her head. 'My husband doesn't sleep with us. He comes back so late that he just stretches out on the sofa over there.' I was betrayed into asking, 'Is that such a good idea?' Midori looked at me as if I was talking another language. She had, it seemed, jettisoned sex along with everything else she had once enjoyed. I turned to her child who had crawled over for a biscuit and remarked, 'What a lucky boy you are! You are sleeping where a lot of other boys have wanted to be.' For a moment something of the old amusement slid over Midori's face. Then she shook her head and asked what kind of nappies I used for nightimes.

On the way home I found Mrs Abe outside her house. It was early summer and for the last ten days her roses had fallen in a wave over the garden wall. The petals had only just begun to wilt but already she was cutting them back with fierce clips of her secateurs. I never heard from Midori again.